WISHBONE
Behind the Scenes

WISHBONE
Behind the Scenes

by

Denise Noe

BearManor Media
2022

Wishbone *Behind the Scenes*

© 2022 Denise Noe

All rights reserved.

No portion of this publication may be reproduced, stored, and/or copied electronically (except for academic use as a source), nor transmitted in any form or by any means without the prior written permission of the publisher and/or author.

Published in the United States of America by:

BearManor Media
1317 Edgewater Dr #110
Orlando FL 32804

bearmanormedia.com

Printed in the United States.

Typesetting and layout by John Teehan

ISBN—978-1-62933-914-6

*Dedicated to my friend,
film restoration expert Jay Fenton,
and to Dorcas Washburn, whose work as
my therapist many years ago helped
make it possible for me to become a
published author.*

Contents

What's the Story, Wishbone?... 1

A *Masterpiece Theater* For Kids................................... 6

The Wishbone: A Disgression On the
 History Behind a Name.. 9

Back To the Making of a Show 12

Two Casts Tied By One Four-Foooted Star 17

Second Second (that repetition is right)
 Assistant Director Allison Graham 24

Catering To a Canine Star 27

Wishbone Performers Discuss Their
 Performances.. 37

People Who Got Their Breaks On *Wishbone* 43

The Process of Writing *Wishbone* Episodes 45

Safety and Protection for Kid Actors 48

Hair and Makeup... 51

Stunts... 54

When a Stunt Goes Oops! 58

Real Life Attack on Mary Chris Wall! 61

Possible Sex Discrimination 63

Making Music for *Wishbone* 65

About Visual Effects 67

The Work of Video Assist 69

Proper Treatment of Props 71

Awards and Recognition 73

Of Dogs and Humans, Performers Bipedal
  and Four-Footed 78

Wishbone Appendix 83

References 103

What's the Story, Wishbone?

What's the story, Wishbone?
What's this you're dreaming of?
Such a big imagination on such a little dog
What's the story, Wishbone?
Do you think it's worth a look? It kind of seems familiar, like the story from a book.
Shake a leg now, Wishbone,
Let's wag another tale
Sniffing out adventure
With Wishbone on the trail
Come on, Wishbone!

THIS JAUNTY SONG introduces a children's television show called *Wishbone* that debuted on March 23, 1995. A handsome and sprightly Jack Russel Terrier is shown running here and there, sometimes with only a dog collar on his neck and sometimes in colorful costumes. The dog is shown standing on a stack of books, running down a street, gazing through a telescope, peering through a window, and looking at a small sculpted version of himself. The canine is seen with wings attached to either side of him, apparently flying through the air. There is a shot of Wishbone vigorously scratching himself as dogs so often do. Dog paw prints appear against a white background. Wishbone appears to trot across a globe.

Each *Wishbone* episode lasted half an hour and consisted of two separate but linked parts from which it would switch back and forth. There was a realistic, contemporary part of the show that took place in the fictional town of Oakdale, Texas and revolved around a dog named Wishbone, his owner, the teenaged Joe Talbot (Jordan Wall), his widowed mother Ellen Talbot (Mary Chris Wall), and other people in his neighborhood and at his school. There was another part of the show that we saw through what the song called the "big imagination" of the little dog. That part told a story from classic literature, myth, fairy tale, or legend. The episode always began in the contemporary segment. The segments were linked through Wishbone who is seen as "just a dog" by people in the modern segment but whose "thoughts," voiced by actor Larry Brantley, are heard by the audience. The concept of the show is that the dog is magically familiar with classic stories of various sorts. He thinks about what is going on with Joe, Ellen, and others in the Talbot orbit and is reminded of something from a famous novel, short story, play, fairy tale, legend, or myth. Then Wishbone takes the audience into a segment in which that is acted out. In the fantasy section, Wishbone is in costume and plays a major character—often, but not always, the hero—and the other characters do not see him as a dog, but (usually) as a human, and react to Brantley talking as Wishbone's classic character talking. There was a segment about African folktales in which Wishbone did not become a human but a legendary "spider." The sight of a dog in a spider costume was a delightful case of cuteness overload! The central plot device of having something in the modern world remind Wishbone of something from a classic helped to underline the perennial relevancy of the classics.

Wishbone was most frequently played by a Jack Russell Terrier named Soccer although there were other dogs of similar appearance who also played Wishbone. The main Wishbone substitute actors were Shiner, Slugger, Bear, and Phoebe. These dogs might perform stunts that Soccer was unable to perform or at which they were just better than he was. For example, Soccer disliked being in water so Phoebe, who took to water well, often did swimming scenes. "She loved to swim, jump, and run," Rick Duffield, the show's creator, commented. "When we needed action, we might go to Phoebe or Slugger. Soccer is more of a close-up dog. He's a hero if ever there was one." Although Phoebe frequently took over when a script called for Wishbone to swim, Soccer was well able to dunk his head in water to retrieve items. Shiner, Slugger, Bear, and Phoebe—or a toy dog—were used for rehearsals, saving Soccer's tricks for the actual filming.

Most commonly, Wishbone was the protagonist of the fantasy segments but he could also be in a secondary or supporting role. For example, he never took the star's role if it was a story built around a female character. "We did not place him in the part of a female hero simply because we felt that might run the risk of mocking a female hero," Duffield explained. He continued that having Larry Brantley "put on a higher-pitched, feminine voice" might be viewed as disrespectful. Thus, in the episode entitled "Bone of Arc," Wishbone did not play Joan of Arc but a friend of hers, Louis de

Conte. Wishbone was also unlikely to be cast as the main character if that protagonist was a fool or villain. For example, Wishbone did not play Don Quixote but sidekick Sancho Panza. Similarly, he was not the divided protagonist in the *Dr. Jekyll and Mr. Hyde* segment but his friend, Gabriel John Utterson.

Perhaps it was in homage to the program's role as an introduction to the great books that, in the contemporary story, Ellen Talbot was given a job as a reference librarian. Several other characters regularly appeared in the contemporary story. Living next door to the Talbots are Joe's close friends David Barnes (Adam Springfield) and his parents, Nathan Barnes (Alex Morris) and Ruth Barnes (Maria Arita). Something of a whiz kid, David hopes to become a scientist when he grows up. His high-spirited little sister, Emily (played by Jazmine McGill in the first season and Brittany Holmes in the second), often gets into mischief. Another close friend to Joe is lively, athletic Samantha "Sam" Kepler (Christie Abbott) who loves soccer (the sport with a small "s" rather than Soccer the dog playing Wishbone), roller hockey, photography, and acting. Her parents are divorced and her Dad, Walter Kepler (Bob Reed), owns and manages Pepper Pete's, a popular local pizza restaurant.

Quirky neighbor Wanda Gilmore (Angee Hughes) is president of a historical society and publisher of a local newspaper called the *Oakdale Chronicle*. Wanda is sometimes exasperated by Wishbone who—he *is* a dog, after all—may dig up her cherished flower beds. Wanda is in a romantic relationship with English teacher Bob Pruitt (Rick Perkins). Joe, Sam, and David all take classes with "Mr. Pruitt."

Kid conflict is often triggered by Damont Jones (Joe Duffield, son of the show's creator, Rick Duffield), an arrogant bully who may cause problems for Joe and his pals. Damont's cousin, Jimmy Kidd (Jarrad Kritzstein), appears in the show's second season and is also a troublemaker.

A *Masterpiece Theater* for Kids

RICK DUFFIELD CONCEIVED the basis for *Wishbone*. He told his staff he wanted to create "a show for kids that was told from a dog's point of view." He had grown up watching the classic TV show *Lassie* and cherished fond memories of that program as well as the loving and resourceful collie who was its star. "I had for some time wanted to do a show that I could sit down with my kids and watch something worthwhile," he recalled in an interview for *Texas Archive of the Moving Image*. "I was convinced that something from a dog's point of view would work for kids." Duffield elaborated that he is enamored of a quote from Samuel Butler: "The great pleasure of a dog is that you can make a fool of yourself with a dog and not only will he not scold you but he'll make a fool of himself too. Duffield had long made it a practice to imagine a voice making statements appropriate to his dog's expressions. He happened to be gazing at his bookshelf when his eye alighted on Frank Magill's *Masterpieces of World Literature*. Duffield wondered, "What if a little dog with a big imagination could take us into some of the greatest stories ever told? And why not make him the hero?"

Thus, the seed for a children's version of the famous BBC series *Masterpiece Theater* was planted. (Duffield's "little dog" and "big imagination" made it verbatim into the *Wishbone* theme song.) Duffield believed it vital to produce a program that would be enjoyable to children even as it introduced them to the classics. He wanted it to be an "entertaining way for kids to get their first taste of great books." Duffield added, "We believe this show can cultivate a new appetite for reading by making kids think it's fun to get to know these books. And it's intended to be fun, action packed, clever, and a way to get their first taste of great stories that can become a valuable educational stepping stone in their lives. The dog makes it all the more endearing and entertaining."

At the time he first envisioned the show, Duffield worked for Lyrick Studios, a company based in Allen, Texas. Duffield went to Lyrick owner Dick Leach and pitched the concept. Leach thought the idea worthwhile and believed it would make an excellent PBS series. Stephanie Simpson, a playwright from New York, came in and acted as head writer plus producer. "I came to Texas to help create the show and come up with the concept and write the pilot script and the show Bible and pitch it to PBS," Simpson said. Prior to writing for *Wishbone*, she had never written for television. As a result, she scurried to a Borders bookstore where she bought a book on the art of writing screenplays. This experience has led her to give this advice to aspiring entertainment industry workers: "I tell any young person, 'Say yes on Friday and figure it out by Monday.' That is the way to live your life in this business."

Betty Buckley was *Wishbone's* producer. In an interview with *Texas Monthly*, Buckley recalled that the concept went through several different hypothetical incarnations before the final basic concept was sketched out. "Rick held some mini-creative conferences on this idea," she explained. "At one point, we were going to have a bulldog that lived in New Orleans." There was considerable discussion about what to call the canine star. "Wishbone was going to be named Knuckles," she wryly recalled. "And Tim Cissell [co-author of *Wishbone* theme song] made his big appeal, like, 'You cannot call the dog Knuckles.'"

Of the name the dog was given, Stephanie Simpson explained, "The idea is that he was a lucky dog named Wishbone. Whenever you got close to him, he made good things happen for you."

The Wishbone: A Digression On the History Behind a Name

Why would the word "wishbone," a nickname for a bone in the skeleton of a bird, be associated with good luck? Ah, here we can "wag another tale."

What Americans have called the "wishbone" since the 1850s is technically called the "furcula," from the Latin word for "little fork." The furcula is made of the joining of a bird's clavicles at the base of its sternum. Although non-flying avians like chickens and turkeys possess furculas, the furcula probably evolved to make flying possible as furculas both hold and release energy when flying birds flap their wings as they soar through the air. (Some dinosaurs also possessed furculas).

The association of this structure with luck goes back thousands of years. The ancient Etruscans believed bird parts could be used to predict the future. "Whenever the Etruscans slaughtered a chicken, they would harvest its wishbone and set it out in the sun to dry (in hopes of preserving the chicken's divining powers)," writes Rebecca Katzman for *Modern Farmer*. "Passersby would then pick up the bone in order to hold it in their hands and softly stroke it while making wishes upon it."

The Etruscans passed this belief onto the Romans when the latter civilization absorbed the former. The tradition of breaking a furcula for luck came about, Katzman continues, "because of a supply and demand problem: So many Romans wanted to make wishes upon the chicken's furcula that there weren't enough wishbones to go around"—unless they were broken in two! The practice of breaking these bones traveled from Rome to its colonies including the ancient island of what is now England. Of course, the descendants of the colonized English, when they became colonizers, brought furcula breaking with them to Plymouth Rock. Since turkeys were native to the "New World," the tradition changed from breaking the furcula of a chicken to breaking that of a turkey.

The tradition of breaking a turkey wishbone after a Thanksgiving dinner persists to this day although specific aspects of the practice vary. In a Thanksgiving article for the *Star Tribune*, reporter Kim Ode quotes one informant asserting that the breaking must "only use pinkie fingers" and another stating that only the "flat tips" of the bone may be grasped. It is generally agreed that the bone must dry after being pulled out of the turkey with some families actually keeping a bone for a full year and breaking it at the following Thanksgiving. Some let it dry until the breaking ceremony is performed at Christmas and others speed drying up via the oven and break it soon after digging it out of the turkey. Many are not picky about drying the bone and just break it after separating bone from surrounding meat.

Since the practice of two people breaking a wishbone as a kind of contest is common, there are varying views as to the best ways to break it to get the larger part of the bone since that is, after all, what constitutes "winning." In an article for the *Star Tribune*, reporter Kim Ode quotes Elmer Sprick as recalling that wishbone breaking contests in the large family of his childhood were "spirited competitions" in which "the ones with the longest arms" were typically victorious. "I soon learned that if one holds the thumb against the upper part of the wishbone during the break, he or she will get the opportunity to make a wish." Joan Donatelle told Ode that the secret to a winning break is to "hold it higher up near the point where the two sides join." Ode reports that an article in another publication advised grasping the bone's limb "between your thumb and forefinger as close as possible to the base of the V" and allowing "your opponent to do the work."

Modern Farmer advises people to ensure their hands are dry, "grasp the wishbone between your thumb and your forefinger, and as close to the center point as possible," and be sure to hold it in your dominant hand and use your nondominant hand to "press back against the counter or some other nearby surface."

Since wishbone breaking is a well-established American tradition and its association with good luck firm in the popular imagination, Wishbone as a dog's name is a sure winner.

Back To the Making of a Show

DUFFIELD DECIDED TO PRODUCE a pilot for the children's TV series he envisioned. One of his first tasks was finding the right dog to play Wishbone. Some dogs are handsome or pretty and some dogs are ugly but even the ugliest of ugly dogs is in its own way "cute." Simply having a dog prominent in a program gives it a certain advantage for this reason. It was important that the dog who would star in Duffield's program be one that viewers would enjoy looking at and that the dog have an impressive array of tricks. It was also vital that the dog be healthy, friendly, and appear emotionally expressive.

During the summer of 1993, between 100 and 150 well-trained canines auditioned for the role of Wishbone. "We looked for quite a few weeks for the right dog," Duffield said in an interview for *Texas Archive of the Moving Image*. The base for these auditions was a Marriott Courtyard in Santa Clarita Valley in California. "I felt like I wanted a small dog but I didn't know what kind," he commented. "I just knew that I'd find the dog if I saw it." At the audition, Duffield recalled, "An extraordinary little Jack Russell named Soccer walked up and dazzled us all." Betty Buckley said it was important to "find a hotel that had grass" since dogs "mark stuff."

Soccer was the last dog to audition. His trainer, Jackie Kaptan, was not with him because she had to work on another show. Another trainer, with whom Kaptan was friends, was there to help the dog demonstrate what he could do.

"I suppose convincing someone that it was a good idea came down to executing a pretty fetching dog trick!" Duffield said. Soccer displayed a friendly and enthusiastic personality. He also displayed a wide range of tricks. The one that particularly impressed Duffield and his associates was a perfectly executed backflip. They were also impressed by his expressive face and his usual attitude of regal calm. "He had this look," Duffield commented. "It was a calm, almost Zen look." Soccer had natural talent, "a certain magic" in Duffield's words, and those talents had been developed into outstanding skills thanks to his experienced dog trainer, Jackie Kaptan. Journalist Kristin Hunt reports that Kaptan "was a seasoned dog trainer who also coached the Dobermans that chase Arnold Schwarzenegger in *True Lies*."

The specific breed of the dog may well have been a major plus for the show. Jack Russell Terriers descend from dogs bred in the early 1800s by Reverend John Russell, a Christian minister who was also a hunting enthusiast and bred these dogs for fox hunting. The Jack Russell Terrier is a relatively small dog that has a white coat typically broken by brown, black, and tan markings. This breed tends to be energetic, healthy, and intelligent. Their high energy level carries dangers as they can become easily bored and a Jack Russell Terrier that is not appropriately exercised and trained can become destructive and even dangerously aggressive. However, if they are well-socialized and appropriately trained, they can be good and obedient dogs. Fans of the Jack Russell Terrier like the way they take to dog sports like flyball and agility. People who especially like this breed typically relish the friendliness of its well-trained members.

Prior to the show *Wishbone*, other Jack Russell Terriers made their mark in the entertainment world. Nipper, a dog that appears to have been of this breed, was the model for the dog Francis Barraud painted in the famous classic painting named *His Master's Voice* that depicts a canine looking into a phonograph. In Great Britain, a Jack Russell Terrier named Chalky appeared on a cooking show with chef Rick Stein. Chalky had his own fan base and lines of merchandise, including the namesake ales Chalky's Bite and Chalky's Bark. Jack Russell Terriers Moose and Enzo (father and son) took turns playing the dog Eddie on the hit sitcom *Frazier* and, again taking turns, had the starring title role in the motion picture *My Dog Skip* (2000).

Dog trainer Jackie Martin Kaptan adopted Soccer in July 1988 when the pup was only two months old. He was named for the coloring of the spots on his coat that resembled a soccer ball plus his liking of little toy soccer balls. Dry dog food and skinless grilled chicken were his favorite foods. Kaptan noted that not every canine is suited to acting. "It takes a special kind of dog that enjoys it," she pointed out. "Soccer wasn't the smartest dog I've ever trained but he had that willingness to please." Indeed, that strong desire to please his human may have been Soccer's greatest asset.

Rick Duffield told *Texas Monthly* that there was difficulty finding the actor who would serve as the voice for Wishbone. "The agencies were sending me cassette tapes and it was all these very serious actors and they were performing as if they were doing Shakespeare," he stated. "They didn't stop to think about the dog."

Larry Brantley, who landed the part of Wishbone's voice, recalled his *Wishbone* audition as "the weirdest audition I think that's ever been or will ever be." He remembered being given only a few facts about the program prior to his audition. "I didn't know what the dog looked like and they gave [me] the barest of information, 'There's going to be this great kids show with this dog that talks and we want you to come in and we want you to be funny,'" he recalled. "So, I went to the first audition having no idea what to do." Nevertheless, he made a positive impression in that initial audition as he was asked for a second one. "In the callback I actually got to meet Soccer for the first time," he commented. He elaborated that the callback audition lasted about five minutes. Rick Duffield suggested, "Watch the dog and just kind of follow along and see what he's doing right now." What Soccer was doing then was "obsessing over this tennis ball." The canine showed no interest in any of the humans in the room but was focused on the tennis ball. "For some reason I still can't quite understand, I started verbalizing out loud what must be going through the dog's head while he's playing catch with himself," Brantley stated. "It must have gone on for two minutes." Then Brantley got hold of the script. He asked the producers if they were ready for his second audition. "No, that was the audition," producer Betty Buckley informed him. Brantley was disappointed, thinking "I just blew this so hard." Thus, Brantley says, he left that audition thinking, "I can't believe I just did five minutes about a tennis ball." But whatever he did, it was the right thing as he was hired. "What landed me the role [was] the ability to observe and just organically go from there," he concluded in retrospect.

The group decided that there would be no attempt to try to make the dog's mouth move as if it were actually talking. "Computer-generated effects were new [at the time] and very expensive," Duffield explained. It may also be true that such an effort would not have added much since the central concept of the show demanded a suspension of disbelief on the part of the viewer who would know in either case that the dog was not the one really speaking.

A backlot was built on the ten acres behind the office building owned by Lyrick Studios. Warehouse space was converted into a sound stage. "That took all spring into summer," Duffield told *Texas Monthly*.

Each *Wishbone* episode was filmed on two interior sound stages plus one interior backlot. A modern set and a fantasy set were specially constructed for each episode. "We had to continually rebuild the universe from the set," Duffield stated.

Two Casts Tied Together By One Four-Footed Star

SINCE THE SERIES consisted of two parts, it had two casts: actors playing in the realistic contemporary segments and actors playing in the fantasy segments about classic stories. Casting director Rody Kent auditioned people for both acting groups. The ensemble playing in the classic segments were called "The Wishbone Players."

In an interview with this author, Rody Kent recalled, "I had been doing a lot of feature film work and TV series work in Dallas so when they got picked up by PBS, they decided they needed someone with experience in national TV casting so they hired me. I was with them throughout the show's shooting."

Commenting specifically on "The Wishbone Players," Kent says, "We needed a rotating group because there weren't that many actors in Dallas. We had twenty-four really talented classically trained actors in that ensemble. Each week we would audition them for specific parts." For the modern parts, Kent continues, "We sometimes brought people in from Houston and other places. Some of them were classically trained but they had a modern day look. Some of them were not classically trained but they were fabulous actors."

Kevin Page, an actor who played in the "classic story" segments of several *Wishbone* episodes, commented to this author, "The first [cast] was the family and kids; the second cast was a core group of twenty-four classically trained actors that formed the basic 'troupe' that then played the majority of 'classic' roles when Wishbone would flashback into the various stories."

Although there were two casts of human actors, its canine star went comfortably from contemporary to classic settings as he tied the two segments together.

The *Wishbone* casting director, Rody Kent, looked for people who would be believable in a modern setting and for those who would do well in the more fanciful segments.

Christie Abbott was eleven years old when cast to play Samantha Kepler. "I'd already done TV before and had been traveling out back and forth to L.A.," a *Texas Monthly* article quoted her as remembering. "Being on sets was pretty normal for me." Abbott knew right away that there was "something very special" about *Wishbone* and asserted, "The synergy of the cast and crew was pretty immediate." Abbott had previously worked with Ellen Talbot in a TV commercial for J.C. Penney. In that commercial, Talbot had played mother to Abbot's child.

In 1994, Ellen Talbot had been working in Dallas, Texas for six years. She had visited Los Angeles and contemplated moving there permanently. On the plane back to Dallas, she prayed, "Dear God, if I'm supposed to stay in Dallas, I need a lightning bolt with my name engraved on the side." A sort of lightning struck: "I kid you not, the audition for *Wishbone* came the next day."

In an interview with this author, Alex Morris said he got the part of contemporary character Nathan Barnes "through a regular interview process. I suppose because it was a PBS show and not one with a real big budget that they cast locally between Dallas, Houston, and Austin in Texas. In the late 1980s, a lot of shows were cast in Texas."

Bob Reed told this writer that he and casting director Rody Kent knew each other prior to the creation of *Wishbone*. "The casting director knew me very well and requested me to read for Walter," he recalled. "I was the last person reading for the role. I found out a few days later that I got the role."

According to Reed, Jordan Wall did not come to the *Wishbone* auditions for the purpose of auditioning. Rather, he was accompanying his little sister who was auditioning. "They talked him into reading for Joe Talbot and he got the part," Reed elaborated. "He was great, knew his lines, knew his blocking. He was just a regular kid."

The road to playing Nathaniel Bobelesky was rather convoluted for actor Justin Reese. "Through an open call in Dallas in the summer of 1994, I showed up on a Saturday, waited in line for hours, went through a couple rounds of conversation and the line reading (as kids got whittled down at each round) and then performed a small scene on camera," Reese told this author. "I believe there were two or three call-backs. By the end, I was reading for the character of David. Obviously, I didn't get it, but they called me in a few months later to work as a background extra. After a couple of episodes as an extra, they asked me to play Nathanael."

Rick Duffield's young son, Joe Duffield, played bully and troublemaker Damont Jones. However, that was not his first role on *Wishbone*—and far from the first role he ever played.

"I wanted to act and play a role in the show," he told this author. "Prior to *Wishbone*, I was very passionate about acting. I participated in several plays throughout school and was in the Plano repertory theatre. One of my favorite parts was playing Jem Finch in *To Kill a Mockingbird*." Joe Duffield initially auditioned for the role of Joe Talbot but believes "they made the right choice in picking Jordan Wall to play that role." Joe Duffield's first role on *Wishbone* was as the Artful Dodger in the *Oliver Twist* segment. "I was really excited to be a part of the show and worked hard to prepare for it," he recalled. "When they asked me about playing the role of Damont Jones I thought it would be a fun challenge."

Going from a classic role to a modern one on *Wishbone* was unusual and perhaps even unique. When interviewed by this writer, casting director Rody Kent said, "Nobody comes to mind as doing that. Normally, we didn't want to confuse the audience by having that happen."

Joe Nemmers, a member of The Wishbone Players, had varied roles in the classic segments of several *Wishbone* episodes. "I was fairly new to TV and film so my audition for *Wishbone* was one of my first big auditions," Nemmers recalls. "Casting director Rody Kent knew me from having cast me before for a role on *Dangerous Curves*. I read for the Christian role in the 'Cyrano' episode. He went to a callback at which both casting director Rody Kent and director Rick Duffield watched. "We were in a fairly small room," Nemmers discloses. "I did the scene as Christian, reading with Rody's assistant." Two days later, Nemmers received a phone call from his agent with the welcome news that Nemmers had booked the role. "I was so excited!" he comments.

Elaborating on his previously quoted comments, Kevin Page said, "I went through an extensive audition to be selected for the classical players. Then, as each episode got ready to shoot, the Company members would be called in to audition again for each individual role."

Jeanne Simpson, sister of Stephanie Simpson, was also part of the acting ensemble that did the fantasy sequences. "The most fun thing about working on *Wishbone* was the magical group of people and canines that I got to work with!" Jeanne Simpson told this author. Not only did her sister help create the series and write most of its scripts but their mother, Doris Simpson, was both the show's educational director and director of the program's child actors. Adam Felber, who would eventually marry Jeanne Simpson, also wrote several *Wishbone* scripts. His brother, Larry Aeschlimann, worked as special effects coordinator.

"I was cast as part of that group that did the fantasy sequences," Jeanne Simpson states. "It was like being in a theatre company. Each week we would be doing a different play." She notes that this gave her and the others in the ensemble a welcome chance to show off their acting chops. Additionally, there was a special sort of interest because of performing with a quadruped. "As an actor, it was a dream come true to inhabit so many different famous characters from classic literature," she explains. "And then it was hilarious because the leading man was always Soccer, the sweetest and most expressive Jack Russell Terrier alive."

Did Jeanne Simpson have a favorite role? "Although I loved all the parts I got to play, my favorite character was probably Joan of Arc," she answered. "In that episode, my brother-in-law, the late and brilliant Larry Aeschlimann, shot me with an arrow and burned me alive at the stake. As an actor, you don't get a chance to experience those kinds of real effects very often. It was challenging and so much fun!"

Todd Terry acted the fantasy segments of "A Terrified Terrier" (*Red Badge of Courage*) and "The Slobbery Hound" (*The Hound of the Baskervilles*). He also played a part in *Wishbone's Dog Days of the West*, a 1998 made-for-TV movie that was based on *Heart of the West* by O. Henry. "I think they originally had cattle call auditions for 'Slobbery Hound,'" he replied when asked how he got his first part. He played Sir Henry in "The Slobbery Hound" and told this author it was both his most challenging *Wishbone* role and his favorite. "Playing Sir Henry was my first attempt at doing classic literature on film so it was a challenge to be true to a character of the time period," Terry comments. "I enjoyed it most because I was on-set longer and it was the larger role. I think that for any actor, it's fun to play different roles because they afford an opportunity to be creative."

In "The Slobbery Hound," Todd Terry as Sir Henry was chased through a forest, tripped, fell, and lapsed into unconsciousness. "The dog had to wake me up," Terry stated. "They put peanut butter on my face so the dog would lick my cheek to wake me up."

Priscilla Wittman was an extra in two *Wishbone* classical episodes, one in "Fleabitten Bargain" and the other in "Digging Up the Past." Her agent got her cast in both episodes. "Fleabitten Bargain" featured the contemporary characters tempted by a shady deal from a swindler, reminding Wishbone of *Faust*. In a *Faust* sequence, Wittman was among a group of dancing revelers. Like the other partiers, she danced in an animal-style mask. "If memory serves me correctly, I was an animal with an unusually long beak!" she said. "I remember sitting in makeup and having every inch of my hair (which was naturally dark brown) totally sprayed black. After that, it was on to costume and then the mask."

And then? "I believe we were told to dance around in a circle," she answered.

In "Digging Up the Past," Wittman appeared as a "Rip Van Winkle" townsperson. "I remember looking at the scenery and the costumes of the others and taking on the atmosphere of another time and place. It was always fun for me to have the chance to do a period piece! I still have fond memories of working on the set of these two episodes."

Dan L. Burkarth did extra work on three *Wishbone* episodes. Asked how he got the jobs, he answered, "They booked me through my agency." On "Bone of Arc," he played a soldier. "I was just running up and down the castle," he recalled in an interview with this writer. "They had a façade of a side of a castle and we ran up and down an exterior ladder during the shot. It looked kind of like a jigsaw." Burkarth remembers the weather as inhospitable. "It was very cold and most of the cast was very scantily clad," he said. "When the camera was not rolling, we could put on a jacket and gloves but we had to shed them when filming. That is pretty standard." He could not remember the name of the episode but knows he worked on an episode set in ancient times. "I was with a lot of people just standing around and fanning," he remarked. "You might be moving something or picking something up just to have action in the background."

Second Second (that repetition is right!) Assistant Director Allison Graham

ALLISON GRAHAM HAD the repetitive title "second second assistant director" on *Wishbone*. "I got my job on *Wishbone* from an AD (assistant director) named Terri Martin," Graham told this author. "I had worked with her on my first gig, *Dallas: JR Returns*. Terri helped me get into the industry and lied about my experience on the last *Dallas* Movie of the Week (MOW). So it was her tutelage that helped me get the *Wishbone* gig."

Just what did Allison Graham do on the series? "Oh my gosh, I did a little bit of everything," she recalled. "Back then, everything was so rudimentary. Terri had move magic scheduling but in order to do the call sheets, she would give me her Production Bible (what we called the AD book that has everything to do with shooting the show)." She described the Production Bible as having "the Day out of Days (DOOD's), Shooting Schedule, One-Liner—a truncated version of the shooting schedule which all laid out each episode on paper."

Graham had many and varied tasks. "One of my jobs as second second AD was to take the documents needed to outline the next day of the shoot to create the call sheet," she explained. "What I would do was take all of the pages from the book that had to relate to what the cast and crew were shooting for the next day. Each page had to be taken to the photocopier and shrunk down to a size that fit on an 8x11 piece of paper. Of course, this is hilarious to think about now but once I was able to shrink each section down, I would take scissors and cut the sections I needed and glue stick them onto the letter sized paper. This would take quite a while as each day there may be more to shoot so more to shrink and photocopy. It is funny for me to think now about using scissors and a glue stick but I did that every day in addition to being a Set PA."

Allison Graham often worked with *Wishbone* extras. "It was really important to Betty Buckley that everyone on the show had a positive experience," Graham stated. "She was great at explaining her vibe so I carried that into my daily routine: be kind. "I would explain to the extras what the scene was about and what they could expect, restrooms, extra's craft service table, waters—everyone had a great time."

What did Graham find most satisfying about working on this series? "Being able to work with such an incredible crew," she told this author. "The cast was also extremely nice as well as all of the day players. It was the type of gig I couldn't wait to get to every day. It was the kindest of all of people, no yelling, no external loud panic, although I know we had our rush days. Working on the show was like hanging out with your extended family. Family is a good depiction of what it was like to work with the cast and crew. I still have friends from that show and have worked with some of them in one capacity or another throughout my career before I move to Los Angeles."

Graham singles Betty Buckley out for special praise. "I learned so much on how to be a good assistant director and to be kind to everyone," Graham comments. "I owe that to Betty Buckley. She was such an amazing leader and really set the tone for how she wanted her set to run. I remember shooting something larger in L. A. and went into where the extras were being held to explain the scene, what they could expect, etc. and one of the extras (Background Performers) spoke out, 'Wow, we have in L. A. for a decade working as Background and no one has ever taken the time to tell us any of all that.' I flashed to Betty in that moment and was extremely grateful she taught me how best to treat everyone. I was kind of surprised about what that gentleman said, and got a solid impression that folks in L. A. treated people differently based on who and what their role was. I didn't learn those bad habits and that has everything to do with being raised on *Wishbone*. Those experiences made me who I became and I am still grateful to have had the opportunity to work on the show."

Catering To a Canine Star

SOCCER HAD HIS OWN TENT in which he and trainer Jackie would wait for filming. The tent possessed a mobile air conditioning unit that ensured Soccer would be comfortable on hot days. "I could hang out there on the backlot on hot days and that's how I got to know Soccer and Jackie," Nemmors said. The four-footed television star strongly impressed Nemmors. "He was a lovely animal," Nemmors avers. "He was such a beautiful adorable dog just as a dog but he also exuded this calm, almost regal quality in the sense of the way he carried himself. He could have been five times his size—that's the way he carried himself." One of the strengths of the show *Wishbone*, Nemmors believes, is the way "Soccer's personality comes through. He was a trained animal but you don't just see that. You see playfulness in him." Nemmors is convinced that the dog relished the human attention he received. "Soccer was very carefully managed because he was an animal but he did like the spotlight," Nemmors said. "He rose to the moment. He enjoyed being the star."

A series starring a dog must consider the limitations of canine cognition in creating the show. Dr. Gregory Berns is a neuroscientist who has done extensive work on the intellectual abilities of dogs. "Their brains don't have the neural real estate to produce and process language like humans do so what they get out of human speech seems to be a much simpler use of words," the expert comments.

Several *Wishbone* performers have remarked on how they were encouraged to avoid behaviors that could have detracted from the ability of the pooch performers to do their jobs. "The actors were not widely encouraged to interact with the dog on-set unless they were actually filming," Kevin Page informed this writer. "Dogs are easily distracted and the trainers did not want Soccer constantly in the middle of a pet-puddle."

Pet-puddle? "Pet-puddle is a word I made up to describe: when everyone gathers in a tight circle around the cutest dog in the room and continuously pets the dog and makes remarks like, 'Ooh, he's so cute!' and 'What a sweet boy!'" Page explained. "In other words, the kind of behavior most people show in relationship to a dog, but on a film set that behavior becomes distracting and (eventually) overwhelming for a small animal if it happens to them all the time. This was one of the main reasons we were not encouraged to pet or even interact with the dog except when 'in character.'"

Stunt performer Richard Phillips recalled, "When we were around the dogs [referring not just to Soccer but to all dogs who played Wishbone], you had to be very attentive NOT to interact because you did not want to get the dogs off track."

Allison Graham also told this interviewer that people working on the series were warned against too much interaction with the canine actors. "Jackie and her assistant made a kind request to us not to touch the dogs," she said. "She explained that Soccer and his stunt doubles were so trained that touching, petting, or distractions of any kind would interfere with their performances. She was really nice about her explanation which totally made sense once you saw them all in action." However, that should not be interpreted to mean she had no interaction with the show's four-legged thespians. "When I would go to get Soccer for set, sometimes there would be a lag," she elaborated. "Jackie would let me pet Soccer and sometimes he was the only dog there because there weren't any stunts on that day. He was super cute but hilariously like an actual star. He was friendly, of course, but not into being cooed upon or loved on like we do with our own dogs or other dogs even. He was a bit aloof. It was as if he knew he was the star of the show but not into mingling with the 'staff.' Ha ha ha. We really all had so much laughter about that."

Dog trainer Jackie Kaptan had to be informed ahead of time about special dog tricks. "When we had stunts where Wishbone needed to make a big jump over a water element or run through a crowd, Jackie had stunt dogs or doubles that were trained to do those exact tasks," Graham asserted. "We would let Jackie know weeks in advance what we were shooting so she could work with the set designers who would build a rig of what the dog(s) were expected to perform. It took weeks to be exact but we never waited on Soccer or any of his doubles—they were always prepared."

It was important not to demand more from the dogs than they could realistically deliver. At one point, Jackie Kaptan said in her *Texas Monthly* interview, "Rick gave me a list of all these things he wanted and I was thinking, 'Soccer's little brain can only take so much.'" It could be necessary to revise expectations to accommodate the realities of what dogs can—and cannot—learn.

The emotional health of the dog often necessitated separately filming Soccer's acting and that of the human performers who, in the aired show, appear to be directly conversing with him. This was especially true in the fantasy segments. "A dog does not understand that if you are shouting or speaking harshly in a role that you are only acting and not mad at him," Page noted. "So, oftentimes, the human actors would do their close-ups—and their more dramatic bits—in a close-up shot in which the dog was not even on-set." When performers were in fact working directly with Soccer, they were careful not to upset the animal. "We would often not look directly at the dog, particularly if the scene was intense drama, because we did not want to scare the dog," Page remarked.

Thus, in many of the fantasy sequences, Soccer or another dog was acting and doing tricks alone and the dog's actions were spliced into film with those of the human performers.

In the contemporary sections, Wishbone usually appeared as a dog would commonly be seen in real life with no clothing but a dog collar and leash. In the classical sections, Wishbone was often quite elaborately costumed. Rick Duffield praised the show's costume designer, Stephen Chudej, as "an absolute genius when it came to designing Wishbone's wardrobe." Duffield elaborates that the canine costumes "were ingeniously engineered to be very lightweight and to provide great ease of movement." Writer Kate Kelly noted, "In general, the costumes tended to end midbelly, making them much more acceptable for four-legged canines."

However, Duffield acknowledged that one item of clothing provided special challenges: hats. "Dogs tend to shake and scratch a lot, so adjusting Wishbone's hat was a common problem on the set," Duffield explained. "We had a costumer on the set at all times, ready to make adjustments for every take."

Nevertheless, there was no story that had to be skipped because of canine costume requirements. "We always believed Stephen could come up with something that would work," Duffield remarked. "In the movie we made for Showtime, *Dog Days of the West*, Stephen even came up with a way for him to wear chaps."

The human costumes could leave the pooches perplexed. "During the first few weeks of shooting, the dogs seemed to have less trouble with their own costumes than those of the human actors in Wishbone's literary fantasies," Duffield remarked. "Soccer was a bit skittish at first around his human co-stars when they returned to the set from wardrobe, hair, and makeup." Duffield dryly speculated that Soccer's southern California background meant he was used to people in "shorts and T-shirts" which would have led him to wonder about the "crazy wig and hat" that adorned his human co-workers.

Costuming caused problem in the "Cyranose" segment in which Nemmors played Christian to Wishbone's Cyrano De Bergerac. "We had a scene in the midst of the battle in which Christian comes running up to tell Cyrano what's going on and every time I ran up to Soccer, the dog would shrink back," Nemmors recalled when interviewed by this author. "Finally, Jackie talked with Rick and said, 'He's scaring the dog.'" What was frightening the canine? After puzzling over this question, it was realized a two-foot long feather in Christian's hat was scaring Soccer. "If I recall correctly, we removed the feather and I moved very slowly and very carefully toward the dog," Nemmors elaborated.

Costume designer Stephen Chudej is now deceased but his widow, Delia Hejny, told the author of this book, "He was very proud of his work on *Wishbone*" and that the period in which he worked for the show was a "happy time" for him.

Matthew Tompkins played several *Wishbone* fantasy roles including Atlas in "Hercules Unleashed" and the Creature in "Frankenbone." Thompkins recalled, "Most of the roles I had I was interacting directly with Soccer, so I had to make the quantum leap of 'I'm in this incredible costume, on this incredible set, with this interesting dialogue, working with this crackerjack crew,' and I turn to my scene partner, and it's a Jack Russell terrier… in a costume." He added that "once you accepted that," the performer "just treated Soccer like another actor."

An animal actor certainly has special needs but this does not detract from the truth that the animal is in fact an *actor*. "We showed up knowing our lines, rehearsed the scene, and then we shot it," Alex Morris recalled. "The dog was so good and the people who trained him were so good! They guided him with hand signals and sometimes with a little clicker. He would do his trick and hit his mark and then he would get a little food treat." Indeed, Morris states that the dog got his blocking and actions right at a level that made him competitive with the human actors who worked with him. "Nine times out of ten he would get it right," Morris asserts. "Sometimes we'd blow a line or miss a mark but nine times out of ten that little dog was right on the mark. He was terrific! I can't say enough about how good that dog was."

In rehearsals, another dog typically substituted for Soccer so the star would not get tired prior to shooting. "We rehearsed with the stand-in dog while Jackie was with Soccer elsewhere rehearsing the tricks he needed to do," Bob Reed related. "It was basically so we could rehearse with a dog there although the stand-in couldn't necessarily do the tricks Soccer needed to do." Reed definitely had a favorite stand-in pooch: Phoebe, the dog that loved swimming. "She was a doll," he cheerfully asserts. "She was an amazing pup. Just very sweet and friendly. She always wanted to sit in your lap."

Sometimes Soccer's substitute was sometimes not another dog but a facsimile of one. "Working with Soccer was a delight but often I would be talking to a stuffed dog when the camera was just on me," Jeanne Simpson disclosed to this author. "When the dog was in the shot, the trainer would be hidden somewhere right next to me. For *Romeo and Juliet*, the trainer was under my skirt on the balcony with me to keep Soccer looking up."

Like other *Wishbone* performers, Bob Reed was instructed to be mindful of Soccer's special needs. "Animal actors are working with trainers who don't want you to distract them," he noted. "They didn't want us to pat Soccer or make a whole lot of eye contact with him but let him do his thing." According to Reed, Soccer was a more dependable performer when he started out than he was later on. "When we started, Soccer was very good but it seemed to me he wasn't quite as good as the show went on," Reed told this author. "I talked to Jackie and she said, 'You know, he's older now and a dog does his job until he decides he doesn't want to do his job.' There were days as we went on when he started to kind of resist. As dogs get older, they may refuse to do their tricks. It's a tribute to Jackie that she always got him through his paces. As time went on, it looked like he would just sit there and look at her instead of doing the trick instantly like he did at the start. He sometimes looked confused like he was unsure what he was supposed to do. It might take Jackie several times to get him to snap into it and do his job. When he did it, he was amazing."

Each species ages at its own rate. As the series progressed, Soccer may have not had the puppy-like level of energy that he had at the start which could account for his needing extra prodding to do the tricks that came easily to him when younger.

Justin Reese, who played Nathanael Bobolesky, also noted that performers were advised not to overwhelm Soccer. "Usually I just tried not to distract him with any sudden movements," Reese said. "When we weren't filming, playing with him was discouraged so we didn't accidentally build any bad habits."

Jeff Klein, property master for the contemporary segments for the first thirteen episodes of *Wishbone*, related to this writer, "I worked with all the dogs, mostly Soccer. It was fun but it was important to not treat them as pets since they are working dogs and you don't want to distract them from the trainer."

Dan L. Burkarth, who was an extra on three *Wishbone* episodes, believes that the special effects associated with the dogs did much to make the show a joy to watch. "Randy Moore did special effects where he would make it look like Wishbone was flying or create a visual image of him vanishing," Burkarth explained.

Soccer could not have been aware of his celebrity like a person would be but it is likely that he knew the humans around him were interested in him. It is also evident that he enjoyed performing his many tricks. "When we'd come back from a break, we'd see him trotting into the building; his head would come up and his tail would wag, and Jackie would say, 'He knows right where he's at and that he's gonna have to work, and he's really happy to be here,'" Caris Palm Turpen, visual effects supervisor, asserted.

"There were other dogs that did other types of action tricks but Soccer was the star of the show, and boy did he know he was the star," second second assistant director Allison Graham commented. "Super cute but he had his own room on the stage that looked like a kindergarten room with ramps, colored mat flooring, sofas—it was where the animal handlers, Jackie and her assistant, hung out with the dogs for the day when we shot onstage."

Joe Duffield praised all the canine actors as well as their dedicated instructor. "Jackie Kaptan the trainer and the dogs were amazing," he asserted. "It was awesome to see all the different things they were able to do, especially in the book/fantasy scenes. They were so well trained." Talking specifically about Soccer, Joe Duffield remarked, "It's funny to say it, but he was so professional. He always nailed his parts and was so well-mannered."

"Soccer was a pro," Justin Reese stated. "He had eyes only for Jackie, his trainer. He was also an alert and attentive dog, so you had to be careful not to distract him but he followed her signals just fine."

Rody Kent also praised the professionalism of the four-footed star. "Soccer had such a unique look," she said. "A lot of times when we were sitting around eating, the other dog actors would look at our food but Soccer would attend to business. He was a very focused dog." Perhaps this is ironic considering how often Larry Brantley, as Wishbone's voice, talked about getting fed. Perhaps Soccer knew the way to get his treats was through the tricks he performed so he concentrated on those tricks.

Wishbone Performers Discuss Their Performances

"**Mixed Breeds**" was an episode that provided Joe Nemmors with an unusual degree of challenge. In "Mixed Breeds," the fantasy segment was about Robert Louis Stevenson's *Dr. Jekyll and Mr. Hyde.* "It's such a well-known character so it was challenging to do something unique and fresh and make Mr. Hyde interesting," Nemmors stated. There was also a special challenge in playing the dual role, Nemmors observes, because he had to "do two distinct dialects."

Getting that particular role came as a surprise to Nemmors. "There was another actor who read for the role and I thought he would land it," the actor explained. "When I went in for the audition, I assumed I had nothing to lose so I took a risk in reading for it. I went very big and I didn't hold anything back. I was as big and bold as possible." Thus, Nemmors added, "When I booked it, I felt a lot of pressure to be as good as I'd been in the audition."

Playing in the *Wishbone* fantasy segments was especially fulfilling for Nemmors. "I think the greatest gift we had on *Wishbone* was that the show gave you the opportunity to use classical training," the experienced actor relates. "Normally, classical training doesn't come into play on TV."

While playing the dual role of virtuous Dr. Jekyll and vicious Mr. Hyde may have been the most challenging *Wishbone* role for Nemmors, another role was his favorite. He played that role in the episode "Rushin' to the Bone," based on Nicolai Gogol's play entitled *The Inspector General*. "There were many roles in which I had fun but if I had to pick a favorite it would be the Inspector General," Nemmors asserts. "I just felt I had the opportunity to do whatever I wanted and really be very playful with it. It is about a comic who comes into town desperate for money and is mistaken for the Inspector General so he poses as the Inspector General." What about this role made it his favorite? "I just felt I had the opportunity to do whatever I wanted with it and really be playful with it," he answered.

"Rushin' to the Bone" was a special episode because Larry Brantley, the actor who voiced Wishbone's thoughts in the contemporary segments and his dialogue in the classic segments, appears onscreen! Brantley has a cameo as actor "Larry Brinkley." The wryly meta-fictional episode had Wishbone playing in a dog food commercial and Brinkley playing the actor dubbing for him!

Rob Owen reported, "Brantley says he worked six days a week, reading *Wishbone*'s line on-set at the same time Soccer acted out a scene and then going into a recording studio on Saturday to record the dialogue. Brantley adlibbed when the dog made a motion that necessitated comment (for instance, if Soccer's left ear stood up straight for no apparent reason) or to fill time if Soccer hit his mark slightly off-schedule." Dogs will be dogs, even when they are also actors, so the filming went on even if Soccer scratched himself or gave himself a shake. However, it is obvious from the show that film was not used if Soccer happened to take a "bathroom break" (so to speak) while being filmed!

For Kevin Page, playing the Phantom in *The Phantom of the Opera*-inspired episode was his favorite *Wishbone* role. "I had been a lifelong fan of old monster movies and so it was a delight to be able to play the role of the Phantom and leave my mark on it," he relates. "Plus, the makeup was super-cool!"

Page enjoyed doing the series so much he took a "show must go on" attitude when it was tempting to stay home. "I had the flu and a temperature of 102 degrees but worked anyway," he said. "It was one of the days while shooting a battle sequence for the Ivanhoe episode."

Alex Morris enjoyed playing Nathan Barnes. "I liked that Nathan was a good role model," he explained. "He was a good father, a middle-class kind of guy, someone most people can relate to. He was kind of a combination of Bill Cosby from his TV show and Bill Anderson from the old *Father Knows Best* series. He was the type of father whose kids could go to him and talk with him. One time on the show David drove his father's car and broke the mirror. I did the same thing when I was a kid and my Dad was furious! But Nathan Barnes was a patient enough father than he allowed the kid to confess." Were there challenges? "The biggest challenge was not making the character too syrupy or too easy," he answered.

Morris said he once wanted to try a stunt but was not allowed to do so since it was not something that his character was scripted to do. This occurred in the episode about African folk tales. "I was *sooo* envious of the actors who were able to fly!" he explains. "I wanted to get in the flying rig but, alas, they wouldn't let me."

While Alex Morris faced a challenge in playing a character who could be seen as "too syrupy or too easy," Joe Duffield was in an opposite situation when playing troublemaker Damont Jones. "The biggest challenge was playing the part of the villain," he said. "I like to think of myself as a kind and good person and it was a bit of a challenge to play the part in an authentic and genuine way."

Justin Reese told this writer about an interesting preparation for the contemporary segment of "The Hunchdog of Notre Dame" episode. "I had to practice being bad at rollerblading," he disclosed. Reese continued that his rehearsals were limited: "I'm sure we ran lines a few times on-set but—at least for my character—there wasn't much rehearsing."

The role of Nathanael was not especially challenging for the young Reese. "Playing a nerd came easy, maybe too easy," he wryly commented. "I'm sure there were a few deeply dorky things I did on-set that got serendipitously folded into the character. For instance, in 'Hunchdog,' my 'hockey helmet' (actually a bicycle helmet if I recall) was pushed much farther back on my head than it should be. I distinctly remember, as a decidedly non-sporty person, thinking that's how you wore it."

Acting on *Wishbone* was a wonderful experience for Justin Reese. "I genuinely can't think of anything I didn't like," he stated. "It was a tremendously fun time. I was on a professional set, goofing around with other performers, knowing I was on a TV show. I had no idea how popular it would end up being, but that didn't matter at the time."

Just as there can be special challenges with animal performers, there can be special challenges with child performers. The parents or guardians of the minors who acted on *Wishbone* were typically on-set.

Actors who were adults at the time are emphatic that the children who acted on *Wishbone* typically displayed a professionalism worthy of their adult counterparts. "The child actors were as professional as the adults," Joe Nemmors states. "They were not prima donnas." Alex Morris worked with the child actors much more frequently than Nemmors since Morris played in the contemporary segments. Morris also praised their conduct. "The kids were really mature and they got along with the adults," he stated. "There were no tantrums. They were professional and the parents were on-set. I got to know Adam pretty well and that came across nicely in the show."

Bob Reed on his *Wishbone* work: "Walter wasn't a regular but a recurring character. I came in once in a while to shoot a scene. We were responsible for having lines memorized and then it was basically blocking that we had to learn. I went to wardrobe and then makeup." The part of Walter came easily to Reed. "I felt really comfortable as I was the right age and the right type for the role," he said. "Christie Abbott was a doll and we got along well. It was kind of like *Father Knows Best*. Mary, Chris and I were old friends, we'd worked together previously so we were especially comfortable around each other."

Reed continued that the atmosphere on-set but off-screen was conducive to comfortable performances. "There are times you just get tickled and it can take a couple of busted takes," he related to this writer. "We laughed a lot. I appreciated Rick's ability to keep things light and friendly on the set. Rick was laid-back and easygoing."

Irma P. Hall played in one episode, "Digging Up the Past," of *Wishbone*. Her character was Dr. Thelma Brown, an older woman who had spent her childhood in the house in which Ellen and Joe Talbot resided. "I just fit what they were looking for at the time," Hall said about her casting as Dr. Brown. Hall said the theme of the show was very relevant to her own life. "I've always been interested in not only what is going on now but how it got that way." She enjoyed acting in a show designed to educate children. "I was passing on information to young people and this is what I do," she told this writer. "God made me a teacher and He gives me opportunities to teach on state, on film, and in classrooms. He prepared for me for it by giving me grandparents and uncles and aunts who set an example. It didn't seem like acting but what my assignment here on earth is about." Even though she was only on one episode, she relished her brief interaction with the show's star. "We just bonded," she said. "When you come in contact with an animal, animals know when you like them and they like you because you like them."

Joe Nemmors singled out the actor who voiced Wishbone for special praise. "Larry Brantley was fantastic," Nemmors averred. "Larry and I would often just start making up stuff in between takes. We would just start riffing and come up with stuff that was hilarious."

"Because half the show was fantasy, there was a lot of makeup, costumes, and props," Nemmors commented. "The actors did goofy things and made jokes. One of the funniest things that happened was when we did *The Odyssey* and Soccer and I had a stare-down. I was trying very hard to stare the dog down and my eyes started to water. In between takes, on the set, people would start doing stare-downs. The spirit of the show was like being part of a family. It was so special because we all knew we were working on something special."

People Who Got Their Breaks On *Wishbone*

THERE ARE WELL-KNOWN performers who got their big breaks on *Wishbone*. For example, Jensen Ackles, most noted for playing Dean Winchester on the television series *Supernatural*, had a part in the first season of *Wishbone*. Ackles portrayed a teenager with mechanical talent in the episode "Viva Wishbone!"

Kristin Hunt reports, "Amy Acker—of *Angel* and *Dollhouse* fame—showed up in the book fantasy sequences of three different episodes of *Wishbone*." She was Catherine Morland in *Northanger Abbey*, Priscilla Mullins in *The Courtship of Miles Standish*, and the goddess Venus in *The Aeneid*.

Comedian Mo Rocca got a *Wishbone* career boost for his writing work. "Writing on that show meant taking some of the greatest stories ever told—the books I was supposed to read in college but hadn't and which I'm sure you have—and retelling each in a half-hour for kids with a dog in the lead role," Rocca explained in his 2016 Sarah Lawrence College commencement speech. "It was storytelling boot camp." He told a *Texas Monthly* writer, "We had this great base—these classic stories that people keep coming back to over and over again—and we had to distill those to thirty minutes, add a twin contemporary plot that would weave in and out of the classic story, and then see it through the eyes of a dog. It was like some crazy creative writing assignment assigned by a teacher on LSD."

The Process of Writing *Wishbone* Episodes

VINCENT BROWN WROTE the screenplays for several *Wishbone* episodes. How did he become a screenwriter for this series? "I went to Yale and, at Yale, I worked on theater productions with Stephanie Simpson," he told this author. "She asked me to write for *Wishbone*."

Brown authored the *Wishbone* episode *Furst Impressions* that was inspired by the Jane Austen novel *Pride and Prejudice*. This writer is aware that *First Impressions* was Austen's working title for the book that eventually was published under the title *Pride and Prejudice*. However, Brown said that was not the reason for the titling of the episode. "I don't even remember if I knew that when I wrote that episode," he said. He wrote two versions of the episode, the second of which made it onto the screen. "I gave it that title because it is about how we don't understand people when we first meet them," he comments. "I wrote a first version and when I presented it to Rick [Duffield], he said he thought it would make a great PBS movie but we needed to make it different for this show. The first version was a little too mature because it was too much about social relations." However, Brown was delighted to work on an episode inspired by a Jane Austen novel. "I love Jane Austen," he states.

The classic works chosen for the *Wishbone* treatment had to be those that were old enough that they were not subject to copyright infringement laws because they were in the public domain. Having majored in literature at Yale, Brown was very familiar with the classics. "When I started work, they had already done *Oliver Twist*," Brown elaborates. "We were thinking mostly about English novels or novels that were translations from other languages. Because of the conceit of the show, we had to find works that would work well in the Wishbone fantasy parts and in the contemporary parts."

Brown believed it vitally important that the African and African-American experiences be appropriately represented on the series. "We mostly did novels but we also did folktales," he observed. "I wanted African or African-American folktales because there wasn't really a classic African-American novel that was suitable for the show." *Wishbone* is especially near and dear to his heart because he did more than just write screenplays for it. "I choreographed the dance and I'm in it leading the dance of the kids in the African and African-American folk tales episode," he said.

Scripts for *Wishbone* had to be geared to the fact that the show wanted to inform as much as entertain. "A huge part of the show was educational," Brown averred. "We especially wanted to help kids having trouble reading because they couldn't imagine the story so we picked books it was likely they would have to read someday."

What did Brown find was most challenging about writing a *Wishbone* script? "Condensing a giant work of literature into a fifteen minute long story," he replied. "Also, we had to figure out ways to write it based on the things Soccer could already do or that he could be taught to do in a short time." Brown did not usually work directly with Soccer but he often discussed Soccer's work with the trainer to find out what the dog could—and could not—be expected to do. "He had to be very focused," Brown observed.

According to Stephanie Simpson, "The biggest challenge was keeping up the pace with our schedule: reading a four-hundred page book in one night and then trying to figure out what the story was for the dog and another for the kids."

"I was particularly proud of the third or fourth episode I wrote about the legendary story of the origins of the Aztec people and also the story of Our Lady of Guadalupe who is a great Catholic icon of Mexico," Mo Rocca was quoted as recalling in *Texas Monthly*. "That was sort of woven in with a contemporary story involving a Latina grandmother. And my mother is Columbian so that felt very personal to me."

Simpson took special pride in "Dances with Dogs," an episode inspired by a Native American story from the Lakota people. "I wrote to the tribal elders and asked for permission to use that," she said. "The guys who came and played the Lakota warriors in the fantasy story but also who played the drum in the contemporary story were from Oklahoma, from the same town that my grandmother is from." She elaborated that the man depicting a Navajo storyteller in the episode was, in fact, a Navajo storyteller.

Safety and Protection for Kid Actors

THE DEMANDS OF THE SHOW meant that it would have been difficult for the major child actors to attend regular schools. Solution? A school for the child stars was specially created for them. The producers hired a teacher and put together a normal classroom. Adam Springfield, Christie Abbott, and Jordan Wall were in their classroom together. "As part of our schooling, we actually made a *Wishbone* newspaper," Abbott fondly recalled. "We would write articles about the different departments." She elaborated that she got quite an education as a performer. "I remember spending a lot of time with makeup and wardrobe and helping with the wigs and them teaching me how to do weaves and coloring."

The minors were safe and appropriately supervised, producer Betty Buckley maintained. "We had a kind of 'kid wrangler'" who was assigned to hang out with the kids because we needed eyes on them at all times." She continued that "the backlot was just a big foresty area." That area attracted the children but not invariably to good effect as Adam Springfield once found himself in all-too-close contact with poison ivy! Despite that, it was probably overall a good thing that they had access to a natural place as Abbott indicated she and the other kid actors enjoyed "playing in the woods." She asserted that "in between takes we were off being normal kids." The child actors developed genuine friendships and Abbott is certain that "contributed to why it was so comfortable. We were friends, kind of like a brother-and-sister vibe."

Joe Duffield has fond memories of his associations while acting on the program. "I enjoyed the interactions with cast and crew," he told this writer. "I enjoyed getting to be a part of something special with a really good group of people. Our family was heavily invested in the show and it was really cool to be part of it from start to finish. The experience taught me so much about hard work, professionalism, and filmmaking." Friendships with his fellow child actors were a major plus. "We got along really well," he remarked. "Most of the [child] actors [were] homeschooled during filming and there was actually a teacher who was on-set and helped them with school work during that time. In television production there can be a lot of downtime, so we did become very close." He also stated that he got no nasty reactions from playing a frequently nasty character. "I never had any negative fallout from playing that role," he commented. "Back then when anyone recognized me or brought it up it was always positive, which was very cool."

Since minors can legally work fewer hours than adults, second second assistant director Allison Graham was given a unique task of being the "legs double" for Joe Talbot! "Kids can only work so many hours and, inevitably, it was never as long as the shooting needed so we would do all of the scenes with the kids and break during the day so they could get their school hours," Graham related. "Often when they were wrapped, I would dress from the waist down in Joe's clothes and do the close-up action with Wishbone."

Substituting—partially!—for Joe Talbot meant that Allison Graham had to take a special interest in scenes in which he appeared. "When I was not cutting and pasting and glue sticking the call sheet, I was on-set for the rest of the day so I was able to see what the actions of the kids were so when we went back to shoot the close-ups I knew how to repeat the direction," she explained to this writer.

Extras were also a special concern for Allison Graham. "I was in charge of wrangling the extras and much of that show had period piece flashbacks so it was my job to check in the extras and get them through 'the works'—meaning hair, makeup, and wardrobe," she said.

Hair and Makeup

HAIR STYLIST AND MAKEUP artist Gi Gi Coker had been working in the entertainment industry for many years before Betty Buckley and others associated with *Wishbone* contacted her to work on the series. "They knew me from other projects," she stated in an interview with this writer. She told them she was not interested in the job. She told this writer that she feared working with "kids and dogs" would just be too much trouble. She recommended other people she knew to be good in the areas of hair styling and makeup. "I was off doing films and didn't want to work steadily on a TV show," Coker commented. "But they asked me to just come in and give them a half hour. I did and I saw people like Stephen Chudej and others who were tops. I sat down and watched a trailer for the show. After that, I thought there was no way I am *not* going to do the show!"

What precisely was her role? "I designed all hair and makeup," she answered. "I had an assistant and sometimes two or three assistants. I personally did hair and makeup for most of the lead characters."

A lifelong bibliophile, Coker thought it imperative that the hair and makeup of the performers in the classical segments be true to the source material. "I read every book that they covered and did every hairstyle according to the book. I wanted to be true to the literature so I did it according to the period and the descriptions in the books."

Doing hair and makeup for the characters in the contemporary segments was considerably easier. "The contemporary characters were kind of all-American," Coker observed. "Their looks were kind of as-they-were. The kids were hired because of the way they looked so we just kept that look. We kind of jazzed Wanda up because she was eccentric but that was mostly wardrobe that did that." Coker noted that actress Angee Hughes, who played Wanda, "already had the reddish short hair" that perfectly fit the slightly oddball personality of her character.

There were no major conflicts regarding hair and makeup styles for *Wishbone*. "We had a production meeting for each episode," she disclosed. "I had already worked with many of these people in film or commercials. Anything very elaborate I coordinated with wardrobe."

Often the hairdos for the historical characters were not done on the natural hair of the performers. "I had over 200 wigs in the department that we would re-style," she explained. "I had a wall hanging with wigs. Over 90% of the period performers wore wigs."

Gi Gi Coker worked with the dogs. "I had two wigs specifically for the dogs," she stated. "We sometimes would sew hair onto a hat that was then placed on the dog. I had a beard that we used in one episode [Rip Van Winkle] on the dog. Anything to do with styling the dog's hair was done by the dog trainer." There were episodes in which Soccer flaunts a pair of eyeglasses. How does one put spectacles on a dog? "Elastic bands around the back of his head and his ears," she disclosed. These bands were not uncomfortable for the animal. "They were very loose and just there to keep things from slipping, kind of like a soft terry cloth headband around your hair."

Christie Abbott commented on the "brother-sister vibe" she had with the other child actors. Gi Gi Coker indicated a kind of "family vibe" among the entire cast and crew: "During our first wrap party, a couple of the crew got up and sang [and] then some started playing instruments. From then on, at any parties, Michael Haines, the sound man, would just set up speakers and all of us would perform. We were such a talented group."

Stunts

THE FANTASY SEGMENTS were especially likely to require stunts. Richard Phillips worked on several *Wishbone* stunts. "The stunt aspect was very professional and well-executed," he informed this author. "One of the craziest things was when we were supposed to be running towards the castle, with horses among us—we were on foot—and we had to *slow down* because the horses were not running fast enough!" Phillips saw a "funny" aspect in that they were running toward their deaths—or, rather, the deaths of their *characters*—but "were excited about it."

Phillips remembered one especially dangerous stunt "when we blew up a castle wall [a different scene and castle from the previously described episode]." "I had not really worked around explosives before on a military set," he disclosed although he had been a "combat engineer in the military" with jobs that included building bridges and blowing them up. Since he was not among those who set the show explosion he "was really nervous about the person who did." So, what happened? "The explosion came off without a hitch and looked wonderful," he replied.

Working on *Wishbone* was rewarding on multiple levels for this experienced stunt performer. "I met a lot of professional stunt men—Don Pike, Jim Henry, Johnny Cannon—on this show which opened up a future for me and I really would like to thank them for taking me under their wings," he stated. "It was great working on period pieces and how the crew would work with you to help get you into the feeling of being 'in the period.' I guess my favorite person was Barbara [B. Baker] from wardrobe, she was so professional and had such a great outlook on life that it would rub off on you and you would just smile after she did her magic."

Richard Phillips praised the overall conduct of those who made this series. "I felt like a part of the family there," he stated. "The complete production had a family vibe. Everyone was very kind and helpful during the show and I cherish my time on the show."

Jim Henry, a stunt performer Richard Phillips praised, also talked with this writer. "I was hired by the stunt coordinator which is pretty much how all shows work," Henry stated. Henry said he got the job partly because he is "local to Dallas" and partly because the stunt coordinator "knew my abilities."

Henry worked on "Bone of Arc" in which he was "pushed away from the castle wall while on a ladder." How was this accomplished without his getting injured? "We had a crash pad for rehearsals but when we were filming, we hit the ground but I was able to tumble and roll." The crash pad was not used in the filming "because it was being filmed downward so a crash pad would have shown." His character also suffered a wound from an arrow in this episode. "Special effects people put the arrow on a wire so we knew exactly where it was going to go," he stated. "A line like a fishing wire was behind me so the arrow was guided by the line—it's called a 'monofilament' but really is just a fishing wire." Being shot by this particular arrow was unlikely to be lethal: "The shaft was wood, the feathers were feathers but the arrow itself was rubber."

On other *Wishbone* episodes Henry did not perform stunts himself but worked in safety to protect the child actors. The kids were doing rough and tumble type scenes. "I put knee pads and elbow pads on the kids," Henry informed this writer. "I also helped put down a crash pad for their rehearsals." Crash pads are sometimes used during actual filming. "If you are shooting in such a way that the audience won't see them," Henry explains. "Of if you can camouflage them by burying them under dirt or leaves or something. But they were only used in the rehearsals of the *Wishbone* episodes I worked on."

Sometimes animals other than dogs were featured on *Wishbone*. In "Hercules Unleashed," in which Soccer played the title hero (wearing an "I am Hercules" lion-skin coat on his back), Hercules encountered a god who turned into a pond. When Wishbone began drinking from that pond, he transformed himself into a bear that stood up on its hind legs and roared!

Soccer was not in the vicinity when the scene with the bear was shot and neither were any of the human actors. This brief scene was created with the assistance of Jean M. Simpson who runs "The Wild Bunch Ranch," a business located close to Jackson Hole, Wyoming that specializes in training animal actors. According to what Simpson told this author, "We were actually in a plane hangar near the ranch." The film was sent to the *Wishbone* creators. The bear did not roar when the scene was filmed. "Any sound is put in later," Simpson comments.

How did Simpson get the bear to stand on its hind legs in what appeared to be a menacing manner without it actually attacking? "All my animals are trained," he answers. "They know they're going to get a reward so they open their mouths and show their teeth. I put a marshmallow on the end of a stick and he stood on his hind legs and got rewarded."

When a Stunt Goes Oops!

ACTING IN *WISHBONE* was not all fun and games. "We shot outside a lot," Nemmors stated. "It could be 100 degrees and we were wearing heavy costumes, sometimes wigs, and we had to rise to the occasion despite the difficulty of the conditions. He noted that it was very cold when filming the episode inspired by *Treasure Island* and "The Legend of Sleepy Hollow." He elaborated that there was filming at night during the "Sleepy Hollow" episode and "it was cold and damp so it was uncomfortable."

Nemmors ran into genuine trouble in "Sleepy Hollow," in which he played Bran Bones. "I was experienced in Western saddle but not English saddle," he revealed. "They sent me to a stable riding school and I was there eight hours learning how to ride English saddle. I've never been so sore. I had a hard time controlling the horse. When I made a hard turn, the saddle slipped sideways and I came off the horse." As a result of that fall, Nemmors was replaced with a stunt rider for that particular part of a scene. "I was embarrassed and humbled," he admits.

Riding horses has intrinsic dangers and this was evident more than once in the making of this series. Actor

Randy Moore played Don Quixote to Wishbone-as-Sancho Panza. Moore was astride a horse when the horse suddenly reared back. "Randy fell off the horse and was injured," Nemmors remembered. "After that, everyone who worked on the show became hyper-vigilant about riding horses."

In in some cases an unexpected occurrence could be used to positive effect. This happened in "The Canine Cure" episode. "Wishbone crawled into bed with Nathanael—unbeknownst to Nathanael—and slept by him all night until Nathanael woke up, chatted with Joe for a moment, then suddenly saw Wishbone and freaked out," Justin Reese remembered. "In the script, nothing triggered Nathanael seeing Wishbone; he just saw him. But while filming, at 'exactly' the right moment, after my line to Joe, Soccer sneezed! I turned, saw him, and had my freak-out moment. After the director cut, the crew were ecstatic that the happy accident had occurred and it made it into the episode."

Reese revealed to this writer that something unexpected also happened while filming the "Hunchdog of Notre Dame" episode. "The hand that catches the ball during the big finish isn't mine," he said. "We shot that close-up at the very end of a long, hot day and even though they were shooting the ball at me from a ball machine not far away, I just couldn't catch it. I missed it over and over. Finally, someone had the idea to just have the stunt coordinator, Russell Towery, put on my glove and put his arm through the sleeve of my jacket (it was too small for him to wear) and catch the ball. I think he did it on the first take." This led to an interesting conversational tidbit for Reese. "Since Russell was also one of Peter Weller's stuntmen for *RoboCop*, I got to tell people RoboCop was my stunt man."

There can be problems caused by the use of any animal performers since they do not, as a general rule, use restrooms when they excrete. Allison Graham recalled an incident caused by this fact. "We were shooting on the backlot, which was the exterior of the town the family lived at and also where the period pieces for the exterior sets were built," Graham stated. "We were shooting 'Bone of Arc' so we had real horses in front of a castle façade. Over the walkie-talkie I hear, 'Allison, come to set with a roll of paper towels and some cleaning spray.' Being eager and a go-getter, I raced to the exterior set and Terri says, 'Allison, a horse has peed right there'—she pointed to the middle of the set where Soccer was supposed to hit his camera mark, 'Go clean it up.' I looked at her and she flatly looked at me and I just replied, 'Yes, ma'am.' I'm sure you know how much a horse can pee but down on my hands and knees I went and went through more than the full roll of paper towels I was instructed to bring. It was slightly funny then but as the years have passed, I tell that story to anyone I mentor so I have laughed a lot about that moment throughout my years of filmmaking."

Real Life Attack on Mary Chris Wall!

IN AN INTERVIEW with the author of this book, Allison Graham revealed that something truly negative happened to *Wishbone* star Mary Chris Wall during the time period in which the series was being made. "Mary Chris Wall was violently attacked by a crazed fan one night after a shoot," Graham remembered. "I don't think that even made the papers and I might be mistaken about the crazed fan. But I am pretty sure it was someone who knew she was on the show, approached her as she was putting her house key in the front door and violently beat her quite badly."

As might be expected, the entire cast and crew of *Wishbone* were concerned about the assaulted performer. "I remember going to work and we were all brought together and Betty came and told us all what had happened and that Mary would be recovering for the next week or so," Graham explained. "When Mary came back to work, we could all still see the yellow bruising. She showed me a few photos of what the police took and I was beyond startled. Her entire face was black, swollen, still one of the most horrifying pictures of an attacked face I have ever seen. Frankly, I did not know how she was not killed. I know she fought back, but as far as who called the police or aftermath, my memory escapes me. But that was the worst thing that ever happened on the show. However, Mary was such a pro she knew we were shooting all around her and came back as soon as she was cleared. Thinking back now, I cannot even imagine the emotional toll that must have taken on her but she never let it show if it even did bother her."

Possible Sex Discrimination

ALTHOUGH ALLISON GRAHAM'S experience on *Wishbone* was overall very good, she told this writer she had a negative one with an assistant director whom she believes had a sexist attitude that led him to discriminate against her. "When the crew went to shoot the Wishbone movie, he took one of the guy P.A.s because he said they needed extra 'Man Power' which really hurt me a lot at that time," she said. "Of course, it was a challenge for women in film to even be considered as managers which is what the AD track is. It is being set-manager. It was my first TV series, but experiencing direct discrimination for my gender was a really hard pill to swallow." Graham was understandably upset at this arbitrary and biased exclusion. "I felt, 'What, I can do everything on the show here, but you won't let me go to New Mexico?' I didn't say that out loud but that was my core feeling."

Graham also recalled a gender difference of a humorous sort. "Something supremely funny the females on the show realized," she remarked. "All of the comments Jackie and her assistant would use for the dogs were the same commands women used or could use on men. 'Come,' 'Stay,' 'No,' 'Here's your mark,' 'Go get it,' we would use those phrases on the guys sometimes and all howl with laughter."

Making Music for *Wishbone*

MARK MENZA WAS ONE of those responsible for the music on *Wishbone*. "Mutual friends who were working in post-audio—Perry Robertson and Gary French—recommended me to music director Tim Cissel," he told this writer when queried as to how he got his *Wishbone* job.

What were the specific musical needs of this program? "As in any narrative drama, you are underscoring the action and the story as it happens," he answered. "Each cue is spotted—we need music here and need to end it here—where you map out where all the [musical] cues will go."

There was no real conflict about what music would be appropriate for specific parts of the program but it might take more than one attempt to get the perfect sort of musical cue for it. "You might get notes back that say something is not quite the right feel for that scene and Tim was great about saying how it might be better," Menza explained. "Then you would rework a cue or two until it was all approved. The directors would have ideas about what they wanted to hear so you would start there. Tim would be the go-between, translating their ideas into something more concrete for the composers. The show's theme needed to make its way into many of the cues that were in present day. Then the historical sections where we moved to another time were really fun. You would then be charged with scoring in some music period lexicon. It really was an opportunity to write in a specific way and then jump back to more contemporary music language in the present day scenes."

About Visual Effects

It was important for Caris Palm Turpen to take care of her eyesight. Christian Wallace and Cat Cardenas reported, "to lessen eye and muscle stress during the long takes, Turpen wore an eyepatch so she could leave her off-viewfinder eye open." Turpen revealed that filming began with what she calls "old-school techniques" of just shooting on film. After that, she and others in visual effects sat at their computers to create digital compositing. There was much layering with live-action combined with other live-action and both combined with digital compositing. She often worked with the Discreet Logic software system to create the final product that the viewers saw.

One index of the quality of the compositing techniques used by *Wishbone*'s visual effects was that even motion picture industry professionals were fooled! "We had film professionals from across the world calling the studio and saying, "When did you go to England? When did you go to Greece?" Turpen related. The show had not in fact traveled but the digital composites came out to look like they had.

Fiction has been called "inspired lying" and the best of film compositing could be called "inspired fooling."

The Work of a Video Assist

FOR THE LAST TEN EPISODES of the last season of *Wishbone*, Stephanie Neroes worked as a "video assist" on the show. She also worked in the same capacity on the made-for-TV movie *Wishbone's Dog Days of the West*. What exactly does a video assist do? "As a video assist, it was my responsibility to provide a video feed from the camera to a viewing monitor so that the director could watch the scene live while I'm recording to tape," she informed this author. "Then, when requested, I would rewind the tape and replay whatever needed to be reviewed."

What did she find most challenging about this job? "I'd have to say ensuring that video was ready to go at every set-up without getting in the way of the camera/electric/grip departments because the cart was made up of a 19" monitor, tape decks, and many wires, some of which I had to use to plug directly into the camera and plug into power provided by the electricians," she answered.

Neroes said that she was party to a very unexpected occurrence when working on *Wishbone*. "There was one night shoot we had to do in 'the woods,'" she relates. "It turns out in the particular location, there was poison ivy. Some folks couldn't work and some were covered head to toe. I had never been exposed to poison ivy so I didn't know if I was allergic or not. I put on gloves and long sleeves to work but, because I had to be quick with wrapping up wires and moving during set-up changes, I had to remove my gloves. Luckily, I wasn't allergic but I'll never forget that night."

Special problems that were encountered when shooting *Dog Days of the West*. "We filmed on location just outside Santa Fe, New Mexico," Neroes recalled. "We were in the mountains on a set built as a western town. Anyway, one day a tornado warning came through and we saw a funnel cloud. There was nothing we could do but watch because the buildings on-set were fake. We just hoped that it would move on without touching down and that's exactly what happened—thankfully!"

Proper Treatment of Props

JEFF KLEIN WAS PROPERTY MASTER for the contemporary segments of the first thirteen *Wishbone* episodes. "I was hired because I'd worked with Betty Buckley and production designer Chris Henry for years on other shows including *Junior Blues*," he disclosed in an interview with this author. He describes *Junior Blues* as "a kind of precursor to *Wishbone*. Before he made *Wishbone* Rick Duffield had the idea for a show about kids and a dog in a music shop in New Orleans and I worked on the pitch video for it. I also worked on the pilot for *Wishbone*."

Klein believes he was hired because he had a knack that would come in handy on this series. "The reason Chris hired me for this job is that I work really well with kids and animals," Klein asserts. "The fantasy segment didn't work much with kids." What exactly did he do as property master? "I was in charge of everything that you can pick up that doesn't breathe," he wittily replied.

Children and animals are both more limited in the hours that they can work than adult humans. "You have to work for about ten hours but the kids and animals can't work as many so we have to juggle things," he stated.

The job on this series was special. "It was the most fun job I've ever had," he cheerfully asserted. "Part of it was the people, part of it was that we were doing something educational, and part of it was that the hours were pretty good for us working on the contemporary side. The people working in the fantasy segments sometimes worked very long hours but not we who did the contemporary parts."

What did he find most challenging? "The most challenging thing was building a robot for the thirteenth show," he answered. That episode was "Frankenbone" in which David builds a robot for his science project.

While the last episode he worked on was the most challenging, it was the first that he suffered a special, and unexpected, difficulty. "I got heat stroke on the first day of production," he disclosed. "We were working outside in the August heat. I was running around and not paying attention to myself so I got a little overheated. I was out of commission for about an hour. Klein added that he was never in any truly serious danger. "We had an EMT [emergency medical technician] on at all times."

After Klein's departure, the property master for the classical scenes, Tom Rutherford, became property master for both contemporary and classical segments.

Awards and Recognition

MANY COMMENTATORS PRAISED *Wishbone* for not sanitizing or bowdlerizing the tales that the program dramatized. For example, in "Bone of Arc" the character of Joan of Arc does indeed suffer a grisly demise by being burned at the stake. However, in a nod to the sensibilities of its young audience, the awfulness is not dwelt on as the camera pans away before fire engulfs the martyred heroine. Commenting on this faithfulness to source material, Larry Brantley stated, "Rick's hard and fast rule is that we don't write down to kids and we do not shy away from difficult subjects." At the same time, the series made sure to stay age-appropriate. As noted, the camera pans away from the burning of Joan of Arc. It also showed sensitivity to its child audience when the story of *Romeo and Juliet* was presented *as a play* so viewers could feel comfortable knowing that both Juliet and Wishbone-as-Romeo were "playing dead" at the story's tragic end.

This wonderful show received appropriate recognition. In 1996, *Wishbone* won the Television Critics Association Awards for Outstanding Achievement in Children's Programming. That same year, the Lone Star Film & Television

Awards made it the winner of its Best TV Program, Movie of the Week, or Miniseries Award. Both victories were repeated in 1997!

Wishbone won an Emmy in 1996 and 1998 for Outstanding Costume Design. 1998 also saw the show win an Emmy for Outstanding Graphics and Title Design, an Emmy for Outstanding Achievement in Art Direction/Set Direction/Scenic Design, and a Peabody Award. The 1998 made-for-TV movie, *Wishbone's Dog Days of the West*, won the 1999 Emmy for Outstanding Art Direction/Set Decoration/Scenic Design.

The "little dog with the big imagination" was popular with its target audience of children, with those who cared for them, and with others. "We received letters from young children, parents, teachers, librarians, dog lovers, and yes, college students," Duffield recalled. The show's inventor was especially pleased that it had done what he so wanted it to do: "Wishbone the dog managed to charm so many people into believing that books mattered. Through his characterizations, kids discovered all sorts of books and story worlds that they may never have known." He elaborated that "librarians seemed to be our most rabid fans." Duffield was also happy that the program was popular on universities. "We were tickled that so many college students liked the show," Duffield recalled. "Some would write us thank you notes for helping them pass freshman lit class." Larry Brantley told a journalist that he met "an entire retirement community in a suburb of Chicago" who were bused in together and "were all fans of the show."

Believing that the show did something good led to a sense of satisfaction for everyone who worked on it. "I think I can speak for everyone who worked on the show when I say that it was one of the most rewarding experiences of our lives to do something that could make a positive impact on young people," Duffield asserted. "To that extent that any young person's life was enriched by what we did is both awesome and humbling at the same time."

On the website DVDizzy.com, a reviewer praised *Wishbone* as "a great time" and observed that the series "was widely seen and clearly enjoyed by many."

Common Sense Media is a guide for parents about children's television shows. One of its reviewers, Ellen Dendy, noted that parents need to know that there were aspects of the series that might make it inappropriate for some children. "Parents need to know that some kids may be bored by parts of this literature-centric live-action series," Dendy wrote. "Some scenes include mild violence—punching, swordfights, etc.—but there's never any bloodshed." She elaborated that "the simple script makes some of the non-fantasy scenes seem fake." Dendy praised the overall thrust of *Wishbone*: "Each episode teaches a key life lesson, and the human characters are good role models." She also stated that "the fantasy sequences are engaging" and lauded the show as one that "encouraged kids to read and introduces them to classic books." Dendy also remarked that is was "hard to resist Wishbone" as he is "so darn cute."

Nancy Warren, another *Common Sense Media* reviewer, wrote specifically about the "Bone of Arc" episode when she observed that this episode "begins with Samantha's friends David and Joe convincing their soccer coach (David's Dad) to let Samantha on the team to save them from defeat." Warren continues about how this leads Wishbone to think about Mark Twain's book on the famous Joan of Arc. Warren states, "While Samantha struggles to kick the winning goals for the soccer team, Joan of Arc, with trusty pal Louis, played by Wishbone, marshals troops to defend France from invading England." Warren pointed out, "The creators also demonstrate their thoughtfulness by revealing the trick of how the actress Joan of Arc is 'shot' with an arrow at the end, thus relieving fears of younger viewers." Warren was impressed that the episode "reminds us of the original super role model for women, Joan of Arc."

Writing for the *Deseret News*, Jessica Messmann stated, "I grew up as an enthusiastic *Wishbone* fan.... Even after it was taken off the air, my friends and I would reminisce lovingly about the dear little dog with an obsession for food and fine literature." She notes, "Most of the novels featured in *Wishbone* episodes are above the reading level of most viewers. However, the little dog compels children to be intrigued by and familiar with the stories, so when they are old enough they will delve into the books on their own." She further observes that the series underscored the truth that the classics remain always relevant by making parallels between their stories and modern "real-world experiences." She ended her article by stating, "*Wishbone* also teaches fundamental lessons like honesty, charity and hard work. Plus, the dog's acting ability never fails to amaze me."

Participating in this series is regarded as an accomplishment by those who worked on it. Todd Terry, who played minor roles in two episodes and also acted in the made-for-TV film, said, "It was a great cast and crew. Larry Brantley really brought the character of Wishbone to life." Terry is certain the concept was helpful. "I thought it was an amazing way to teach kids, and adults too, about history and literature."

Kevin Page enjoyed a strong sense of satisfaction in working on *Wishbone*: "I was always rather proud of the fact that we were teaching kids to love reading (and imagination) which was something I loved to do as a kid (and still do)."

"It was one of the most fun shows on which I've worked," Rody Kent told the author of this book. "We had great camaraderie. We just had fun. People had a good time. We couldn't wait to see the next story were would be telling. We all loved introducing classical literature to kids. It was an honor and a privilege."

Allison Graham asserted, "I still have some incredible friendships [made on *Wishbone*] that last today. I was a better AD, Line Producer, and Producer/EP because of my early experiences [on *Wishbone*] and I would not trade a moment."

Of Dogs and Humans, Performers Bipedal and Four-Footed

NO ONE KNOWS for sure when and where the ancestors of a now extinct species of wolf evolved into dog. Nor do we know *how* the process of domestication took place. This writer's favorite scenario is what follows.

Wolves began hanging around early human camps in search of food scraps. Most wolves were not terribly successful at getting bits of nourishment from humans because they feared humans and were aggressive toward humans so humans feared them and tried to stay away from them. There is variation in every species and some wolves were below the norm in fear and/or aggression toward humans. These wolves were more successful in getting scraps. These more successful—because less fearful of people and/or less frightening to people—wolves had more pups that inherited their characteristics and were in turn even more successful at getting their hunger met by humans. Among these wolves were some that retained more puppy-like appearances with such features as large eyes. They reminded humans of their own young so humans began actively tossing unneeded food to these wolves. Eventually, these successful characteristics became more and more common among certain of these wolves until a wolf birthed a puppy that was not a wolf but the first dog.

The process may have taken thousands of years. But its end result was a species—the dog—that was symbiotic with the human species. For just as the humans helped physically nurture the dog, the dog emotionally nurtured the human. Each species became dependent on the other. Just as the dog is man's best friend (man understood in this sense as "human" rather than male), so is the human the dog's best friend.

Anthropomorphism is always a danger in discussing other species. Dogs must be understood and appreciated for what they are which is very different from what we humans are. One of the most obvious differences is in the importance of specific senses in understanding our environment. Humans tend to be visual creatures with hearing the second sense source and smell a distant third. By contrast, dogs live in a world of smells with their olfactory sense far more developed than ours. Dogs fail the "mirror test" for self-consciousness. No matter how long a dog sees its reflection, it never realizes it is looking at itself rather than another dog. However, this does not necessarily indicate an absence of self-consciousness since vision is not nearly as important to dogs. A researcher found that his dog spent less time sniffing something with his own urine than that of other dogs. This could indicate that the dog recognized the urine as his own which could suggest consciousness of self. It is also possible that the dog was familiar with the odor of his own urine so he was less interested in it.

For many animals, the emotions possible are quite limited. The main goals of the majority of species are to eat and avoid getting eaten. Thus, their emotions are largely limited to fear, contentment, and aggression. However, dogs have a relatively wide and rich collection of emotions. Current scientific studies tend to indicate that our canine friends have mental abilities and emotions similar to that of human children at about age two and a half. In addition to fear, contentment, and aggression, they experience excitement, distress, anger, joy, suspicion/shyness, and love. Beyond the dog's emotional possibilities are the emotions of shame, pride, guilt, and contempt. Some dog owners interpret that shrinking that dogs often do when they have torn something or had an excretory accident in the house as guilt or shame. It is fear as making oneself as small as possible is necessary in the wild to protect oneself. However, it is likely that dogs make themselves small because they fear a reprimand. In an article about dog emotions, Stanley Cohen cheerfully notes, "The good news is that you can feel free to dress your dog in that silly costume for a party. He will not feel shame, regardless of how ridiculous he looks."

Applying what we know about canine cognition and emotions to the dogs who did their part to create the lovely television show called *Wishbone* can help us understand what the four-footed thespians experienced. Realistically, we should realize Soccer never actually knew that he was the star of a TV show. Phoebe, Shiner, Slugger, and Bear never knew they acted in a television show. But what they did know was that when they did certain tricks the humans around them were happy. Even if they were not "proud" of their accomplishments in the same sense a human might be, it is likely they experienced joy at the pleasure they brought to their trainers and to the other two-legged creatures who lavished attention upon them. It is also important to note that while Soccer probably did not experience shame or guilt, he was well able to *act* those emotions. A trick he had done pat, that of putting a paw over his eye area, perfectly conveyed feelings of shame and/or guilt.

The dogs knew that they did good and they liked doing good even if they were unable to appreciate the complexities of that goodness. However, the readers of this book can appreciate it as do the many who have watched *Wishbone*. Michael Brody reported in his book *Seductive Screens: Children's Media—Past, Present, and Future* that Rick Duffield "lamented" that "only fifty episodes were filmed, all in a one-year timeframe"—although they aired in a three-year timeframe with a year without new episodes airing. Brody elaborated, "PBS halted production because *Wishbone* did not have 'merchandising potential'" and was not "toyetic," a term "attributed to a Kenner toy company executive in describing *E.T.* to Steven Spielberg."

However, this writer believes it is fine that the show ended when it did. TV shows are not meant to last forever. This was a show oriented toward children and its child actors were approaching adulthood. Dogs are elderly when they hit their teen years so it was good to retire Soccer, Phoebe, Shiner, Slugger, and Bear before they became sickly with old age. They deserved a rest before they died. Fifty enchanting, inspiring, and educational episodes are a powerful achievement. *Wishbone* enhanced and enriched the childhoods of many youngsters. It continues to do so through reruns.

For centuries, a wishbone has been considered lucky. Who can guess for how many years *Wishbone* will bring its special brand of good luck to appreciative audiences?

Wishbone Appendix

Episodes of 1995

"A Tail in Twain: Part One"   March 23, 1995

The Talbot family, like others in the neighborhood, are preparing for the annual neighborhood picnic. Ellen Talbot says, "It's my turn to say something about my life in our neighborhood." Joe, Sam, and David want to learn about the neighborhood cemetery's mysterious "No Name Grave." Wishbone is reminded of Mark Twain's *The Adventures of Tom Sawyer*.

"A Tail in Twain: Part Two"   March 24, 1995

Continues and winds up the stories of the "No Name Grave" in the contemporary segment and of the funerals of the very much living Tom Sawyer and Huckleberry Finn in Wishbone's literature segment.

"Twisted Tail" Oct. 9, 1995

A hungry Wishbone finds his food bowl empty and is reminded of the hungry orphan in Charles Dickens' *Oliver Twist*. Back in the modern segment, Joe, Sam, and David befriend a newcomer to the neighborhood, Max. Wanda discovers that a pink flamingo decoration is missing from her yard and wonders if Max could be the culprit. Joe, Sam, David, and Max talk with a cocky kid who shows off his roller blades… or *are* they *his* roller blades? Wishbone-as-Oliver encounters the Artful Dodger. Wanting to find the thieves, David crafts a camera that the kids place on Wishbone, making him a kind of detective "cyber-dog" who captures on film the evidence required to nail the thief.

"Rosie, Oh, Rosie, Oh!" Oct. 10, 1995

Entranced by a dog of the other gender named Rosie, Wishbone is reminded of William Shakespeare's *Romeo and Juliet*. The classic story is presented in the episode as a play on a stage with Wishbone, of course, the handsome and debonair Romeo. After the play ends, Wishbone appears on stage with the other performers to take final bows.

"Homer Sweet Homer" Oct. 11, 1995b

"Dognapping in progress!" is what the audience hears as it sees Wishbone in a cage being pulled by Emily through a park. The situation reminds Wishbone of the part of Homer's *The Odyssey* in which Calypso tries to keep Odysseus on her island. David and others remonstrate with Emily for trying to steal Wishbone. The kids learn that much of their beloved park may be destroyed by Mr. King, a real estate developer. Returning to the fantasy segment, we see how Penelope has tried to stave off her many suitors and how she worries about the fate of her son, Telemechus, in a house overrun by her would-be grooms. Wanda and the kids launch a petition drive to save the park, especially its 200-year-old tree.

"Bark That Bark" — Oct. 12, 1995

The kids assist in a storytelling program as a fundraiser with David's Uncle Homer telling African folktales. Wishbone plays major roles in fantasy enactments of the folktales including one in which he is the trickster spider Anansi. Uncle Homer also tells the story of how legendary Africans grew wings and flew. Wishbone appears to have wings and flies gracefully through a sky that is rich with fluffy white clouds. Uncle Homer relates that when the slave traders came for them they could not take their wings but they could, and did, bring their wisdom. After the show proper ends, there is a brief discussion of how flying was simulated through flying harnesses.

"Cyranose" — Oct. 13, 1995

Wanda brings a sculpture to Ellen and reveals it was inspired by Wishbone. The art piece reminds Wishbone of the play *Cyrano de Bergerac* by Edmond Rostand. The kids sweat over a school poetry assignment with David, whose forte is science and the laboratory, having special trouble. David's. Wanda reminds David that he is a "good student" but the encouragement does not seem to affect David. In the fantasy segment, Roxanne becomes exasperated by the tongue-tied Christian. When she is away, Christian says to Wishbone-playing Cyrano: "If only I had your wit." Cyrano replies: "If only I had your looks." Then Cyrano feeds Christian eloquent lines. Back in the contemporary story, an anonymous poem is suddenly and mysteriously delivered to David. He passes "The Birds of My Backyard" off as his own to a very impressed Mr. Pruitt. However, conscience later gets the best of him and he confesses the truth. Mr. Pruitt wants to find the gifted author of the beautiful poem which leads to his meeting Wanda—the start of a romance that will persist through the series.

"The Slobbery Hound"   Oct. 16, 1995

A dog is causing destruction in the neighborhood. Wishbone is unjustly blamed and sees a parallel to Sir Arthur Conan Doyle's *The Hound of the Baskervilles*. Animal Control officers issue a $150 fine to the Talbot family—but they have time to contest it. The episode goes back and forth between Wishbone-as-Sherlock investigating the legendary "curse" of the Baskerville family and Joe, David, and Sam investigating, trying to find the dog that really did the damage to clear Wishbone and save the Talbots' money. The episode ends with a discussion of visual effects and how a photograph of a large manor in England was composited with live action to create the "Baskervilles" scenes.

"Digging Up the Past"   **Oct. 17, 1995**

Wishbone is comfortably on the couch as Joe informs Ellen that he has a school assignment to write on "something our grandparents had that we wish was still around." This reminds Wishbone of *Rip Van Winkle* by Washington Irving. Oakdale is visited by a woman, Dr. Brown, who lived in the Talbot home forty years previously and wants to know if the childhood treasures she once hid could still be in their secret hiding places. The "Rip Van Winkle" segment shows Wishbone wearing a white beard, a touch that gives the episode an extra zing both comedic and dramatic. After the stories end, there is a discussion of how special audio effects were used to make the ghosts Rip Van Winkle met in the mountains sound ghostly.

"Bone of Arc"   **Oct. 18, 1995**

The best player on the school hockey team is sidelined by an injury so Sam offers to substitute. The classic parallel is young Joan of Arc saving France from the English invaders as told in the book by Mark Twain. Transported to Joan's world, we see Wishbone as her best friend Louis de Conte. The teen-aged Joan determines to lead France to freedom and restore the rightful French king to the throne. Sam scores the winning points but the team's victory is voided on a technicality. *Wishbone* shows Joan of Arc as captured and tells of the unfair trial that led to her burning at the stake. However, her example inspired the French to ultimate victory. Just as France was eventually victorious, people are proud of Sam despite the fact that the team's win cannot technically count. "You can lose a battle but win the war" is the moral.

"The Impawssible Dream" Oct. 19, 1995

Joe wants to make a world record for basketball shots. Wishbone dreams of *Don Quixote* by Miguel de Cervantes. Wishbone appears as sidekick and squire Sancho Panza. Ellen reminds Joe of the math homework he needs to do but Joe is focused on that record like Don Quixote is focused on battling the giants that Sancho Panza knows are windmills. Damont shows up to try his hand at making the world record. Not everyone can be a record setter just like Don Quixote cannot be a knight after the age of chivalry has passed.

"Fleabitten Bargain" Oct. 20, 1995

Wanda tells Ellen and Joe about "The Historical Society Crafts Fair." Bob Pruitt will not be able to help her so Joe will become her assistant. Wishbone thinks about the legend of Faust as interpreted in the play by Johann Wolfgant von Goethe. Wishbone-as-Faust is seen in hat and spectacles poring over one of a many of a multitude of books. His yearning for loving companionship plus adventure brings the devil into the room with a dirty deal. At the crafts fair, Wanda spots a modern day snake oil peddler selling a "wishomatic." Will the devil get the soul of the all-too-gullible Faust? Will Joe barter Wishbone for a wishomatic? After the stories end, there is a discussion of how light and dark were used in the filming to represent good and evil.

"Sniffing the Gauntlet"   Oct. 23, 1995

Mr. Pruitt divides the class into two teams for a spelling bee. Sam, known to love reading, is made captain of her team. Wishbone is reminded of the competitions between Normans and Saxons in Sir Walter Scott's *Ivanhoe*. The episode does not get into the issue of anti-Semitism that was a major part of the novel but only tells the viewers that Isaac of York and his daughter Rebekah were "outcasts" without giving the reason for that status. As the kids prepare for the second day of the spelling bee, disaster strikes: Sam has an allergic reaction to the coconut in a snack. This is paralleled to the injury Ivanhoe suffers. During a contest, Wishbone-as-Ivanhoe is derided as a "dog of a Saxon!" The stories end and there is a brief discussion of the making of the show's "castle."

"The Hunchdog of Notre Dame"   Oct. 26, 1995

Nathaniel Bobolesky is introduced as a character. He is a kid who is athletically clumsy and is ridiculed for it. Wishbone dreams of Victor Hugo's *The Hunchback of Notre Dame*. Costumed with a conspicuous hump on its back, Wishbone portrays the tragic but heroic Quasimodo.

"Golden Retrieved"   Oct. 27, 1995

A new bicycle absorbs Joe's attention, leaving him little time for Wishbone who fantasizes about George Eliot's *Silas Marner*. Wishbone gets lost and Joe realizes that his focus on his bicycle led him to ignore the dog he loves. Silas Marner obsessively counts his gold only to lose it all when it is stolen. But one form of gold is replaced with another when a golden-haired child demands his concern. Joe and Ellen are distraught when they realize Wishbone is missing and even Wanda Gilmore participates in the search for the missing dog.

"A Tale of Two Sitters" Oct. 30, 1995

David comes over to the Talbot house accompanied by sister Emily and her little friend Tina. David is supposed to be babysitting but her leaves the younger children inside the house while he and David go outside to play. Wishbone is reminded of *A Tale of Two Cities* by Charles Dickens. Wishbone plays the role of the aristocrat Charles Darney who runs afoul of the French revolutionaries who blame him for the wrongs done by his family. Emily and Tina get into mischief. Charles Darney gets into jail and the shadow of the guillotine. Following the stories, there is an explanation of the role of the foley artist in adding sounds after filming and ensuring the sounds correctly match the visual action.

"Frankenbone" Oct. 31, 1995

Joe is gluing "fossils" together for his science project while David wants to keep his project a secret. Wishbone is reminded of *Frankenstein* by Mary Shelley. David's science project, like Dr. Victor Frankenstein's, is a humdinger that gets away from its creator. The episode ends with a discussion of the makeup used to make an answer look like the famous creature stitched together and brought to life by Dr. Frankenstein.

"Hot Diggety Dawg" — Nov. 1, 1995

It's Arbor Day! Wanda persuades the kids to dig a hole for an Arbor Day tree planting, leading Wishbone to think of *Journey to the Center of the Earth* by Jules Verne. Complete with wire-rimmed spectacles and backpack, Wishbone looks scholarly yet adventurous as Professor Otto Lidenbrock. In the contemporary story, Wishbone decides to show Wanda and the kids how a real digger digs and he digs up a mysterious round artifact. The discussion that follows the stories focuses on how the *Wishbone* art department used Styrofoam to craft caves as well as how the crew generated explosions and created clouds of smoke.

"One Thousand & One Tails" — Nov. 2, 1995

The kids experiment with a new computer. David, the computer whiz, discovers a conversation among thieves. Wanda's purse gets lost and Emily grabs it. Wishbone fantasizes himself into Scheherazade's *Arabian Nights*. Flaunting a narrow beard and sometimes riding a donkey, Wishbone plays Ali Baba.

"Mixed Breeds" — Nov. 3, 1995

Wanda finds herself intrigued by a dashing rock and roll performer in the local pizzeria. Will the debonair and dramatic singer lead her away from Bob Pruitt? Wishbone thinks about Robert Louis Stevenson's *Dr. Jekyll and Mr. Hyde*. Wishbone is not Jekyll/Hyde but friend Gabriel John Utterson.

"The Canine Cure" Nov. 4, 1995

Nathaniel Bobolesky stays at the Talbot residence but Wishbone must stay in the yard and not come into the house because Nathaniel's mother informs the Talbots that he is allergic to dogs. Wishbone dreams of Moliére's *The Imaginary Invalid*.

"The Pawloined Paper" Nov. 6, 1995

Joe writes a love note to a teacher on whom he has a crush. Another kid knows about the note and plans to get it and advertise it to the school so Joe tries to retrieve it. The fantasy parallel is Edgar Allan Poe's "The Purloined Letter" with Wishbone visualizing himself as detective C. Auguste Dupin. Wishbone makes a dashing detective.

"Bark to the Future" Nov. 14, 1995

Joe is doing poorly in math. This disappoints Ellen who will not let him play on the basketball team if his math grade is too poor. He hopes a calculator will help him make better math scores and Wishbone fantasizes about the H. G. Wells novel, *The Time Machine*. Wanda holds a yard sale and Joe sees the vital importance in math as Wishbone is torn between the Eloi and Morlocks of the future.

"Paw Prints of Thieves" Nov. 8, 1995

A cafeteria worker and Joe defy the orders of the cafeteria

director by taking leftover food—that would otherwise go into the dumpster—to a homeless shelter. Their attempts at charity remind Wishbone of the legend of Robin Hood with the dog, quiver full of arrows on his back, playing the expert archer, master of disguise, and hero of the forest.

"Furst Impressions" Nov. 9, 1995

Damont asks if Joe and his friends are going to the school dance—and if they will have dates like the "cool" kids. Joe becomes self-conscious about his clothing when Damont criticizes it. Wishbone is reminded of the dancing at the balls in Jane Austen's *Pride and Prejudice*. Rumors fly and harm in both segments. Wishbone as Mr. Darcy shows off his formal dancing skills.

"The Prince and the Pooch" Nov. 10, 1995

Joe thinks he would be a better coach than the actual coach. Wishbone is transported into Mark Twain's *The Prince and the Pauper*. Learning how the other half lives can be a humbling kind of education.

"The Count's Account" Nov. 13, 1995

David builds a machine and Damont causes mischief. The classic parallel is Alexander Dumas's *The Count of Monte Cristo*. The stories are followed by a discussion of the importance of sound effects in cinema.

"Salty Dog"   Nov. 14, 1995

Wanda shows Ellen and the kids "The Trumball Barn," a barn condemned to be destroyed. She tells them a legendary horseshoe might be in the barn. The kids hope to find that horseshoe. Wishbone fantasizes about *Treasure Island* by Robert Louis Stevenson with the dog taking the role of Jim Hawkins. Following the stories is a brief discussion of making a new barn look old and how the burning of a little toy barn was used to make it look like a real barn was burning.

"Little Big Dog"   Nov. 15, 1995

Ellen and Joe Talbot leave on a trip and ask David's family to dog sit. David's Mom scolds him for breaking a vase. Then Emily owns up to breaking it. Wishbone fantasizes about the Biblical story of David vs. Goliath. Wishbone plays the Biblical David. Emily learns that she listened to her conscience in confessing to breaking the vase. David tries to drive Mom's new car and causes a mirror to fall off. Will he find the courage and conscience to confess? A discussion of the importance of music in shows follows the stories.

"A Dogged Expose"   Nov. 16, 1995

Someone has been leaving pictures of Sam with her mouth open and finger close to her nose around the school. Sam, David, and Joe try to figure out the culprit. Wishbone once again daydreams his way into being Sherlock Holmes, this time in Sir Arthur Conan Doyle's "A Scandal in Bohemia."

The trio suspect Amanda, Sam's frequent rival, but learn that Amanda is the victim of a similar trick. This puts Sam and Amanda on the same side as they try to figure out who would be mean enough to do this. Wishbone-as-Sherlock also aims to unmask a phony, playing with the show's central conceit along the way with lines like "I would test myself against any—dog—in England" and "My nose for clues."

"A Terrified Terrier"   **Nov. 17, 1995**

Joe is flattered when an older boy known for his basketball skills, together with his circle of pals, takes an interest in him. Joe neglects Wishbone as well as best pals Sam and David. Wishbone transports into *The Red Badge of Courage* by Stephen Crane with Wishbone playing another "young man in a hurry" soldier, Henry Fleming. Joe realizes that he could lose his old friends. Wishbone-as-Henry Fleming gains a "red badge of courage" in battle. The discussion that follows the stories reassures young viewers that there was no danger to any person—or dog—in the Civil War scenes.

"Shakespaw"   **Nov. 20, 1995**

In this singularly inspired episode of a singularly inspired show, the stories shift from a school play of Shakespeare's *The Tempest* to Wishbone's imaging of *The Tempest*. In the contemporary segments, Amanda plays Ariel; in the fantasy segments, Wishbone is Ariel. Wishbone has never looked more flamboyantly beautiful than he does in his Ariel costume.

"Muttketeer!"   Nov. 21, 1995

In the contemporary segment, Wishbone as "stealth dog" seeks the rat (of the four-legged variety) that has been chewing up items in the kids' school. In Wishbone's fantasy, he is d'Artagnan in *The Three Musketeers* by Alexandre Dumas. The fantasy segment is distinguished by energetic and obviously skilled fencing and Wishbone wearing a narrow mustache.

"Hercules Unleashed"   Nov. 22, 1995

Sam's Dad is about to celebrate his 40th birthday and Sam wants to get him a good gift. Wishbone is reminded of Hercules and the fabled quest for the golden apples.

"Viva Wishbone!"   Nov. 23, 1995

Joe and Sam are hanging up something welcoming back "Senora Julia." Joe, Sam, David, Ellen, and Wanda are welcoming this close friend back to Oakland from her annual visit to her family in Mexico. She brings Joe a book entitled *Legends of Mexico*. Ellen has been helping a youth who lost his own mother, triggering jealousy in Joe. Senora Julia tells him about Juan Diego and Our Lady of Guadalupe. Wishbone plays Juan Diego. Discussion follows about how important murals are to storytelling in Mexico and how a mural was composited into live action in this episode.

"The Entrepawneur"   **Nov. 24, 1995**

Joe starts a grocery delivery business and finds that a single-minded and selfish focus on earning money could cost him his friendships with David and Sam. Wishbone is reminded of the legend of King Midas and his golden touch as related by Ovid's *Metamorphoses*.

"Pantin' at the Opera"   **Nov. 27, 1995**

A magazine article lavishes praise on Ellen Talbot for her computerized library cataloging system. Then the library is the site of mysterious doings, including the seeming appearance of the previous reference librarian - - who retired ten years ago and whose widow wrote a letter Ellen read saying he died months ago. Wishbone thinks of *The Phantom of the Opera* by Gaston Leroux. Wishbone is not the Phantom but Raoul, Viscount de Chagny. The formally attired Jack Russell Terrier looks distinguished as he carries a red rose in his mouth to his ladylove.

"Dances with Dogs"   **Nov. 28, 1995**

This episode reinforces a point made in some past episodes: stories are not always found in books. Native Americans are an example of peoples with rich oral traditions of storytelling. Native American storyteller Lee Natonabah tells the stories of his people and Wishbone transports himself into a warrior in a Native American tale that Natonabah relates.

"Rushin' to the Bone" Nov. 29, 1995

Wishbone is a finalist in the contest to act as "Mr. MacPooch" in a dog food commercial. The fantasy sequence is about Nikolai Gogol's *The Inspector General*, a comedy about mistaken identity. Wishbone plays Osip, valet to the civil worker Khelestakov who is mistaken for the Inspector General. At the Mr. MacPooch auditions, a dog auditions who is named Knuckles, perhaps a nod to a name once suggested for Wishbone.

"Picks of the Litter" Nov. 30, 1995

Wanda leaves a dog that belongs to a friend with the Talbots. Wishbone entertains fellow canine with stories taken from the fantasy segments of prior episodes.

EPISODES OF 1997

"Halloween Hound: The Legend of Creepy Collars: Part 1" Oct. 15, 1997

It is Halloween and Oakdale is full of carved pumpkins. Ellen wants to know if Joe will go trick or treating. He spots an old house that looks spooky and happens to have a black cat coming out of it. Wishbone thinks about "The Legend of Sleepy Hollow" by Washington Irving. The dog plays Ichabod Crane.

"Halloween Hound: The Legend of Creepy Collars: Part 2" Oct. 16, 1997

Wind-up of the first part. This two-part episode is wonderful as it is genuinely quite spooky, wonderfully funny, and—as usual—educational. A discussion of the use of darkness and lighting by the crew follows to explain the eerie look achieved in this two-part episode.

"The Prince of Wags" Oct. 16, 1997

Joe is elected basketball team captain and Wishbone is transported into William Shakespeare's *Henry VI Part 1* as Prince Hal with the parallel that both must learn qualities of good leadership.

"Groomed for Greatness" Oct. 23, 1997

Wishbone is selected to model for a statue sculpted by Wanda's artist cousin. The fantasy goes into *Great Expectations* by Charles Dickens. Wishbone plays Pip. Discussion follows of how special effects created the fire in *Great Expectations* without endangering anyone.

"A Bone of Contention" Oct. 30, 1997

Joe yearns to ask Sarah to the dance but cannot find the courage. He requests that David do the asking. Then Sarah and David find themselves in a mutual admiration club, leaving Joe feeling left in the lurch. Wishbone fantasizes he is John Alden in *The Courtship of Miles Standish* by Henry Wadsworth Longfellow.

"War of the Noses"   Nov. 6, 1997

Wishbone is taken to the vet, Wanda accidentally sends the dog's chair to be reupholstered, and Joe must deal with a kid who tells fanciful stories he does not admit are not true. The classic segment is about *Black Arrow: A Tale of the Two Roses* by Robert Louis Stevenson in which Wishbone plays Richard Shelton. Discussion follows about Soccer's stunt doubles Phoebe, Bear, Slugger, and Shiner.

EPISODES OF 1998

"Moonbone"   March 7, 1998

Under the full moon, Wishbone is seized by a desire to bury everything he can. Sam gets accused of stealing a ring she photographed. Who really stole it? Will it be recovered? The fantasy segment is about *The Moonstone* by Wilkie Collins. Wishbone is the handsome and distinguished Detective Franklin Blake.

"Barking at Buddha"   March 13, 1998

Younger neighborhood kids yearn to hang out with older kids. Wishbone sees himself as an ambitious character,

"Monkey," in Asian legends. Discussion about combining elements of traditional Chinese design and making a stage full of brightly costumes and masked people looking like it was amidst the clouds.

Also on March 13, 1998, a feature length made-for-TV movie entitled *Wishbone's Dog Days of the West* was aired. In this film, Wanda Gilmore catches a clue from Wishbone which leads her to an action that saves the the life of a child. She is acclaimed a hero! However, the good publicity is soon overshadowed by negative publicity when she is the target of an investigation depicting her as the "town tyrant." In the fantasy segments, Wishbone is transported into O. Henry's *Heart of the West* in which Wishbone is Long Bill Longley. Will Wanda clear her name? Will Long Bill Longley, together with pal Tom Merwin, save a town from the scoundrel Calliope Catesby?

"Pup Fiction"   **March 25, 1998**

Wishbone wants to learn who has been sending Wanda anonymous letters. The fantasy segment is a telling of Jane Austen's *Northanger Abbey* with Wishbone as Henry Tilney. A discussion of the importance of costumes in historical stories follows.

"The Roamin' Nose"   **April 1, 1998**

The neighborhood is evacuated due to a gas leak. People spend time mulling over their pasts and becoming better acquainted with each other. Wishbone is transported into Virgil's *Aeneid* with Wishbone playing (who else?) Aeneas. The episode gives insight into Damont Jones who has lived in the shadow of an elder brother's accomplishments. There is also a sense of reconciliation with a new friendship between Damont and Joe.

References

The author thanks the following people for allowing her to interview them: Allison Graham, Joe Nemmers, Justin Reese, Rody Kent, Vincent Brown, Kevin Page, Jeanne Simpson, Bob Reed, Todd Terry, Gi Gi Coker, Alex Morris, Priscilla Wittman, Dan Burkarth, Richard Phillips, Stephanie Neroes, Jeff Klein, Irma P. Hall, Jim Henry, and Jean M. Simpson.

Cardenas, Cat; Wallace, Christian. "Top Dog: An Oral History of 'Wishbone.'" *Texas Monthly*. Oct. 2020.

Coren, Stanley. "Which Emotions Do Dogs Actually Experience?" *Modern Dog*. Winter 20/21.

Dendy, Ellen. "Wishbone." *Common Sense Media*.

Eskin, Blake. "The Exchange: Rick Duffield." *The New Yorker*. Oct. 21, 2009.

Handwerk, Brian. "How Accurate Is *Alpha*'s Theory of Dog Domestication?" *Smithsonian Magazine*. Aug. 15, 2018.

Hanks, Robert. "Fall of the wild: a brief history of dogs on film." *Sight & Sound*. Aug. 11, 2015.

Hare, Brian; Woods, Vanessa. "Opinion: We Didn't Domesticate Dogs. They Domesticated Us." *National Geographic*. March 3, 2013.

Hunt, Kristin. "11 Classic Facts About *Wishbone*." *Mental Floss*.

Katzman, Rebecca. "What's the Story, Wishbone?" *Modern Farmer*. Nov. 26, 2014.

Kelly, Kate. "Wishbone, Dog TV Start." *America Comes Alive!*

McGowan, Kat. "Did humans truly domesticate dogs? Canine history is more of a mystery than you think." *Popular Science*. Feb. 10, 2020.

Messmann, Jessica. "'Wishbone' a brilliant TV series." *Deseret News*. March 27, 2011.

Miller, Adam. "Dogs may be smarter than we think—and can benefit our health in ways we don't realize." *CBC News*. Dec. 7, 2019.

Ode, Kim. "No bones about it, breaking the wishbone is a family tradition." *Star Tribune*. Nov. 26, 2014.

Owen, Rob. "Release the Hound: *Wishbone* Creators on the Show's History—and Its Uncertain Future." *Paste Magazine*. July 27, 2020.

Texas Archive of the Moving Image.

Warren, Nancy. "Wishbone: Bone of Arc." *Common Sense Media.*

"Wishbone, Dog TV Star." *America Comes Alive!*

"Wishbone" DVD Review. DVD and Blu-ray Reviews.

Wishbone. Internet Movie Database.

Worrall, Simon. "Dogs Have Feelings—Here's How We Know." *National Geographic.* Sept. 9, 2017.

www.ingramcontent.com/pod-product-compliance
Lightning Source LLC
Chambersburg PA
CBHW072201160426
43197CB00012B/2480